"Kristen Howerton's authority, brilliance, wit, and wisdom is exceeded only by her authenticity. When Kristen writes, I pay attention because not only am I challenged and informed, I am becoming a better person in the world. This book is one part therapist, one part best friend, and such a gift to a generation of women tired of the mommy wars."

—SARAH BESSEY, author of *Jesus Feminist*
and *Miracles and Other Reasonable Things*

"Kristen is refreshingly candid, sharply funny, and deeply self-evaluative in her storytelling about everything from infertility to adoption to introversion to racism to faith to dismantling the patriarchy. Kristen's authenticity will inspire you to stop obsessing over the perfection-oriented optics of parenting so you can opt out of the 'shoulds' and opt in to the stuff that truly matters to you." —CHRISTINE KOH, PhD., co-author of *Minimalist Parenting*
and co-host of the *Edit Your Life* podcast

"Kristen Howerton transcends genre, fusing populist and literary sensibilities to communicate her essential message of inclusivity and tolerance. Both provocative and compassionate, Howerton brings her unique brand of humor to some of the most sensitive and explosive subjects facing our society today, including faith, race, the shifting paradigm of family, and radical self-acceptance. She is a personal hero of mine, and I count her among the voices I turn to in my moments of deepest soul-searching, as well as when I just need a killer recipe for homemade mac and cheese or a great place to find a stylish sofa on-the-cheap. She's a national treasure, and her memoir is a sorely needed beacon of light in these dark times."

—JILLIAN LAUREN, *New York Times* bestselling author of *Some Girls: My Life in a Harem* and *Everything You Ever Wanted*

"Kristen Howerton is a good writer with ideas worth reading. Family, love, friendship, relationships and her escape from the restrictions of simplistic religion are just some of the themes she addresses with humor and clarity. Howerton is a welcome voice for sanity and compassion counted on by millions of readers worldwide."   —FRANK SCHAEFFER, *New York Times* bestselling co-author of *Keeping Faith*

"Kristen Howerton is a powerful voice in the movement to take back motherhood and make it fit our real lives. Her wit, humor, and authenticity are unmatched, and her writing wins every day."

—CLAIRE DÍAZ-ORTIZ, co-author of *Hope Runs: An American Tourist, a Kenyan Boy, a Journey of Redemption*

RAGE AGAINST THE MiNiVAN

CONVERGENT · NEW YORK

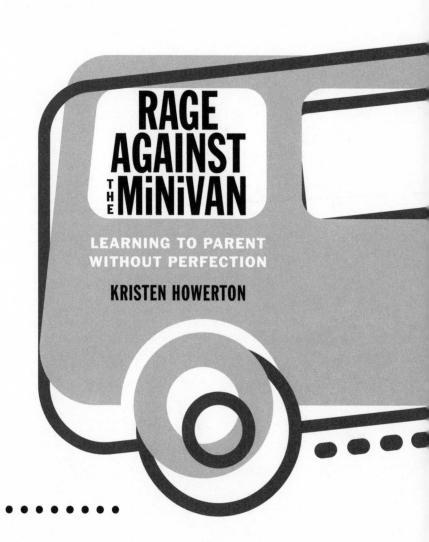

RAGE
AGAINST
_{THE}MINIVAN

LEARNING TO PARENT
WITHOUT PERFECTION

KRISTEN HOWERTON

Published in the United States by Convergent Books, an imprint of
Random House, a division of Penguin Random House LLC, New York.

crownpublishing.com

CONVERGENT BOOKS is a registered trademark and its C colophon is
a trademark of Penguin Random House LLC.

LIBRARY OF CONGRESS CATALOGING-IN-PUBLICATION DATA
Names: Howerton, Kristen, author.
Title: Rage against the minivan / Kristen Howerton.
Description: First edition. | New York: Convergent, [2020]
Identifiers: LCCN 2020003348 (print) | LCCN 2020003349 (ebook) |
ISBN 9781984825162 (hardcover) | ISBN 9781984825179 (ebook)
Subjects: LCSH: Howerton, Kristen. | Motherhood. | Motherhood—Humor. | Parenting.
Classification: LCC HQ759 .H78176 2020 (print) | LCC HQ759 (ebook) |
DDC 306.874/3—dc23
LC record available at https://lccn.loc.gov/2020003348
LC ebook record available at https://lccn.loc.gov/2020003349

Printed in the United States of America on acid-free paper

2 4 6 8 9 7 5 3 1

First Edition

Time-line graphic on page xi by Robin Plemmons

Book design by Debbie Glasserman

TO JAFTA, KEMBE, INDIA, AND KARIS

*In the midst of the sarcasm, I hope
this reads as a love letter to the
adventure of being your mom.
It's been the best ride of my life.*

CONTENTS

Dear Reader,

If you are looking for a parenting book with great craft ideas, amazing time-management tools, and motivational inspiration to do more each day, then awesome. *There are a lot of those books out there. You should google them.*

This is a book about doing less.

Which is ironic. Because anyone who knows me knows I really like getting things done. I struggle daily to abandon the ideal of the perfect mother who "does it all."

My learning curve as a parent was complicated and difficult. While trying to become a mother, I battled infertility, recurrent pregnancy loss, and adoption drama. Then I had kids, and I battled anxiety, perfectionism, exhaustion, a constant feeling of being overwhelmed, and a crisis of purpose. I still battle those things. But along the way I've learned some lessons about letting go.

I hope this book will give you permission to embrace doing less. If you are reading this and don't have kids, I'm glad. Because I wish I'd read a brutally honest account of the emotional realities of becoming a mother before I had kids. Instead I read a bunch of books with advice about using a rectal thermometer and accurately warming up breast milk. While helpful, they did not adequately prepare me for the mental endeavor. Hopefully this book will help you rage against the narratives of motherhood and life and relationships and gender that tell us we aren't enough. And for those of you reading who don't plan to have kids, I will also provide some random thoughts on faith and race and divorce, on Christian code-speak and hating Elf on the Shelf and how hard it's been to make friends in my forties. Life is nonlinear, imperfect, and complicated. This book is, too. My brain, like my Web browser, has too many tabs open at once.

I had four kids in four years, two by adoption, two by birth. Just the other night, I met a new neighbor and when she asked about the ages of my kids, she said, "Wow, you just popped them all out really fast!" And I disclosed that no, actually, it was a convoluted journey. I explained the birth order of my four children, and she said, "I'm having a really hard time tracking this." I reassured her that I feel confused sometimes, too.

So, I'm going to draw you a time line of how I got here on the facing page.

Spoiler alert . . . as much as I raged against it, I lost my battle against the minivan. It now sits in my driveway covered in crushed Cheetos, smelly soccer gear, and remnants of my self-esteem.

1994 — went to Bible College

1995 — Got engaged to a PASTOR

1996 — got married to a PASTOR

1999 — Got licensed as a therapist

2001 — 1st cell phone (NOKiA flip phone, baby.)

2002 — Bought our 1st home

2003 — Started trying to have kids

2004-2005 — the Miscarriage Years

JUNE 2005 — Jafta joined our family at 6 Months old as a foster child

JAN. 2006 — I started a BLOG — RAGE!

Oct. 7 2006 — I gave birth to India & Kembe was born in Haiti

APRIL 2007 — We were matched to adopt Kembe from Haiti

MAY 2008 — Jafta's adoption was finalized at age 3

APR. 26. 2009 — I gave birth to Karis

JAN. 2010 — Kembe joined our family at age 3

May 2013 — Everyone I lived with learned how to wipe their own asses

SEPT. 2014 — EVERYONE IN MY HOUSE WENT OFF to SCHOOL — OYES!

October 2015 — A day I got all of the laundry done & folded

JULY 2017 — Divorce

AUG. 2018 — Accepted pajamas as a reasonable outfit for school drop off

JUNE 2019 — 1st family trip on a plane where no one needed anything from me

RAGE AGAINST THE MINIVAN

THE INTERNET IS FULL OF $*!# AND SO AM I

We have the choice of two identities: the external mask which seems to be real . . . and the hidden, inner person who seems to us to be nothing, but who can give himself eternally to the truth in whom he subsists.

THOMAS MERTON

A couple years ago, NPR reached out to me for a segment they were doing about the holidays. They wanted to interview me for tips on how moms could stay organized and calm in the midst of the season. I said yes, being the NPR nerd that I am, and then promptly forgot to put the interview in my calendar.

I had absolutely no business giving any shred of advice on successfully navigating the holiday season. I have a massive meltdown pretty much every year mid-December. I predictably overbook myself, take on too much, and fail to say no. This particular year was no exception, and my stress was affecting my health. I wasn't getting enough sleep, my immune system was shot, and I had developed shingles, a reactivation of the chicken pox virus that manifests in mind-numbingly painful blisters. Shingles is, according to Google, thought to be brought on by stress.

One morning, a few days after NPR booked me to do the segment, I stepped out of the shower and began applying calamine lotion to the rash across my chest and stomach when my cellphone rang from a New York number. I picked up, thinking it was my agent. An NPR host told me to hold. I would be live in two minutes.

The calamine lotion was still wet so I couldn't get dressed. I turned, and on the other side of the sliding glass door that separates the bathroom from the outside I saw the guy who mows my lawn step into the backyard. I couldn't close the curtains without exposing my body even further, so I scurried into the toilet alcove, which would at least partially hide me from view.

There, naked, with sopping wet hair and covered in calamine lotion while hiding from a man mowing the grass in my backyard, I gave a national interview on how *other people* could stay sane during the holidays, including tips on mindfulness, self-care, and slowing down. I hung up and thought . . . *I AM SO FULL OF SHIT.*

Back in my twenties, I loved to scour through home design magazines for inspiration. Today I am just as likely to peruse Pinterest, home decor websites, or foodie Instagram accounts as I am to read a magazine. The shift from magazines to social media has spawned a marketplace where *anyone* can create inspirational content. I love the fact that the Internet allows creatives to publish their own work. We are looking at real people, real homes, and often, real families. We think.

As a personal blogger, I've been in conversations with many

other bloggers who have noticed this shift. Blogging started out as a kind of online journal, but for many it has morphed into more of an online magazine—little snippets of real life that perhaps don't paint the full picture. It's the highlight reel, and honestly? Sometimes it's very staged.

I've gotten to know enough social media mavens to know that under that perfectly clean kitchen counter is probably a pile of recently cleared junk. I've met the homeschooling mom who has a hired "governess" to teach her kids while she blogs. I know Instagramers who take a week's worth of wardrobe photos at once, with their hair and makeup professionally done, and then post them every day with an #outfitoftheday tag so we think that's how they always look. I know the mommy blogger who takes her kids to open houses and takes photos in those perfectly staged houses to present the illusion that's her life. I've met the blogger who portrays her marriage as amazing and fun while in real life, things are strained and distant. (Oh wait. That last one was me.)

I worry about the false messages about life, and specifically about motherhood, these influencers are collectively sending. Many of the early visions I had for my own family were drawn from images of motherhood presented in curated feeds that highlighted a perfect domestic existence, complete with sun-kissed lighting, designer clothes, and slightly mismatching West Elm pillows. I wanted those aesthetics for my own life. Creating those scenes would make me a good mom.

Then I had children. As it turns out, children arrive with personalities and needs that do not cooperate with our fantasies. My children were more interested in cartoon-emblazoned plastic toys than the artisan-crocheted dolls I bought on Etsy. They preferred SpongeBob to nature documentaries. They turned up their noses at vegetables or any kind of sauce, requesting instead the Bland Beige Food Group. They were uninterested in quiet family meals. Our table felt more like the breakfast scene from *Cheaper by the Dozen* than something painted by Norman Rockwell.

Motherhood is beautiful, but it's also messy. In fact, happy family life *should* be messy. A lifestyle of only perfect moments is not a lifestyle I'm familiar with, nor is it one in which kids can really thrive.

On any given day, my sink is full of dishes. My house is clean exactly twice a month, every other Friday afternoon after the cleaning lady has come. The night before we all do a mad dash to clean the house *before* the cleaning lady comes because most rooms have gotten too messy in the course of two weeks for her to even be able to mop the floor. Most days there is a pile of clean laundry sitting on the sofa waiting to be put away. There is a chair next to my bed that solely exists for me to pile clothes on it. This chair is NEVER empty. I have never sat in that chair.

In the dining room there is a credenza whose sole purpose is being a place to pile papers. About once a month I will go through the papers and realize all of the things I forgot to do/sign/deal with. My junk drawer is so full that you have to rattle it a bit to open it, and every pen in there inexplicably does not work. Despite my daily nagging, there are approximately twelve pairs of shoes scattered across my living room floor, and probably more than a dozen abandoned cups. So many cups, you guys.

As the kids are getting older we also have real-life dramas. Broken hearts and social issues and challenges in school and therapy appointments. We are far from perfect. And yet I think we are very typical. We're an average, okay, mostly happy family. And my ongoing challenge has been learning that this is enough.

It's still a constant temptation to compare my life to the

"highlight reel" people post online. Once I was scrolling through Instagram and saw photos of a friend on a Hawaiian vacation with her kids. And as I looked at their photos, I had this pang of jealousy. I was thinking, *Wow. They really go on a lot of trips. I wish I was able to do that. I want to be a family that travels more. They look like they are having so much fun.*

Then I realized that I was looking at my phone *at an Airbnb in Palm Springs where I was staying with my kids for a week.* I was jealous of someone else's family vacation *while I was on my own awesome vacation.* That is how absurd social media FOMO can be.

The truth is that contentment is an inside job. So is authenticity. Validation doesn't come from magazines, blogs, Facebook feeds, or even your best friends. It doesn't come from looking like you have it all together online. It's easy to spend our time trying to manufacture the visuals of contentment, or longing for the images of happiness that permeate social media. It's harder, but more rewarding, to dig into our own lives to do the work of finding gratitude and satisfaction in our private moments.

The struggle to be content and happy with your imperfect self is a journey. Over the years, I've worked hard at settling into peace with myself as a "good enough" mom, while maintaining some semblance of my own identity outside of parenting. That's what raging against the minivan has come to mean to me. It's the quiet rebellion against obsessing over the optics and outcomes of motherhood, from the kind of car we drive to looking like we have it all together. It's about opting out of the comparison game and giving ourselves permission to fail, to get back up, and to love with our whole hearts again the next day.

POOP, THERE IT IS

Mothers are all slightly insane.

J. D. SALINGER

I was an amazing mother before I had kids.

I had it all planned out. There were meadows involved. There would be handmade wooden toys and organic, home-cooked meals. There would be picnics on hippie-inspired blankets (in the meadows) and vintage books and lazy days at the park (more meadows). There would be crafts of some sort, and late-night family readings of the classics by the fireplace.

I knew the kind of mom I'd be. I would be present and in the moment. I would be fun and carefree. Breezy. And while I would be warm and attentive to my children, I wouldn't lose myself in motherhood. I would strike the balance, be able to focus on my kids while retaining my own identity. I would get my body back quickly. I would keep shopping at Urban Outfitters, but also maybe start to dabble in Ann Taylor because linen would be a good look for my maternal bliss. I would maintain the same lifestyle I'd had *before* kids. I would take my kids to art galleries and they would learn to eat at nice restaurants. I would avoid things like "mom haircuts" and cropped pants. I would be the same me, only with kids. And linen pants.

I also knew what kind of mom I *wouldn't* be. I vividly remember a teenage moment of judgment toward one of my own mom's friends. She had a toddler and a new baby, and we'd gone to her house one evening just after dinner. Her toddler was screaming in a high chair, and the baby was crying, and the house was a mess. My mom's friend was wearing a filthy T-shirt with a large brown spot just above her breast. When my mom asked what happened, she casually mentioned the baby had a diaper blowout. It took a minute for me to register. Then it hit me: SHE HAD POOP ON HER SHIRT. The fact that she was just talking like it was no big deal, instead of running at full-speed to change, completely disgusted me. How could you care so little?

I vowed, there and then, that I would never be *that* kind of mom.

It turns out motherhood was more exhausting than I ever imagined. I looked and felt nothing like the mother I'd thought I would be. I felt tired and frazzled. I no longer recognized the body I inhabited. I didn't have time for things like hair appointments or workouts. Or showers. Going shopping for food felt like an insurmountable challenge, and I may have once started crying in public when there were no double carts left at the grocery store.

It hardly felt like living. I was surviving. It humbled me to discover that the thing I'd always wanted most in life—the thing

I fought tooth and nail to achieve—overwhelmed me every moment of every day. Shouldn't I have been more grateful? Shouldn't I be relishing every moment of this? Shouldn't I be in a state of maternal bliss? WHERE WAS THAT MEADOW??

Instead of feeling comfortable, confident, and awash in baby cuddles, I felt completely unequipped. Frequently, I found myself looking around and feeling like I was the *only* mom experiencing so much chaos. As it turns out, I am not the breezy mom in linen, effortlessly picnicking with her children in picturesque tableaus. I am the mom who forgets water bottles at playgroup, who forgets sunscreen at the beach, who forgets to pack lunch for preschool, and who remembers the helmet as we are pulling up to the skate park. I am the frazzled and sweaty mom who misses appointments and yells more than she'd like to admit. I am the mother who has left baby poop on her shirt way longer than what is sanitary or appropriate.

This became clear to me one day early on, when I had only two kids and attempted to take them for a walk to the beach. This fit my dream of being the kind of mom who took her children to the beach on a whim, packing them deftly into the stroller and burning a few calories on the way there. My oldest child, Jafta, was three at the time. Five days earlier, we had gotten him his first bike. He asked to ride on the path to the beach instead of sitting in the stroller. This sounded like a win-win to me. I could push his baby sister in the stroller while he rode beside us. He was happy. I was happy. Spur-of-the-moment beach days were about to become a regular thing!

Reality hit when I realized there were approximately forty-seven things I needed to prepack in order to make this a successful endeavor. But regardless, I prepared. The kids were sunscreened, I remembered the sand toys and helmet, and I even brought some snacks. I drove us to a parking lot that fed into a bike path about a mile from the beach, giving us a decent walk and ride while taking us to an empty beach spot.

Then things took a bad turn. About a half mile in, Jafta rode his bike through a huge pile of dog poop. Seriously, it was an epic quantity. Poop caked into every ridge on both tires, kicking up as he rode, covering his seat and legs. I was horrified.

I had Jafta dismount the bike. I tried to clean off the poop by running the wheels through the sand. I struck at it with a rock. That poop was going nowhere. *Maybe it will come off as he rides,* I thought. We decided to keep going.

Well, I was right. Poop *does* come off tires as you ride a bike. It comes off in very small pieces that spit up from the tires and hit you and your daughter in the face. So our lovely walk at the beach became a game of Frogger in which I had to dodge a hailstorm of projectile dog feces. Poop lodged itself in my hair. I had to keep my mouth closed to avoid ingesting it. But we carried on, because dammit, we were going to the beach. (Also, I knew a demon-possessed three-year-old tantrum would ensue if we turned back.)

Meanwhile, my toddler daughter decided to play a game of "throw the sippy cup" as we walked. She launched the sippy cup from the stroller in sixty-second intervals. Each time, I retrieved it. Taking the sippy cup away from her was not an option, because that caused her to scream at the top of her lungs. To avoid a full-tilt meltdown, I learned I had to play this game of catch with her while simultaneously avoiding the torrent of dog poop.

Finally, frustrated and literally shit-faced, we arrived at our destination. We headed down to the beach, where there were tons of little tide pools. Now, I have a strict "stay away from the water" policy on these walks because I don't like being outnumbered by two non-swimmers near the ocean. As a result, I hadn't put them in swimsuits for this journey. Wearing regular clothes kept them from clamoring to go swimming, and they were always happy to play in the sand. But today the tide pools looked so welcoming, and my kids looked so excited, and I thought, *What's the harm?*

So my kids started playing in the tide pools, fully clothed. That was when I realized they were getting soaked. Organic cotton may be soft and environmentally friendly, but it does *not* dry well. We were facing a mile-long walk back to the car in wet clothes. So as we finished up, I decided to remove the kids' dripping clothes. You can imagine the result. One child is a diapered baby in the stroller, who had been sunblocked at home according to clothes she is no longer wearing. Her pasty white stomach, arms, and legs are now unprotected in the summer sun. The other child, of course, is a three-year-old prepared to ride a bike in his underwear.

As I am taking in this scene, I am thinking . . . *Surely this kind of thing does not happen to other moms.*

My son climbed back onto his bike in his wet underwear and, it turns out, had about a third of a cup of sand stuck between his butt cheeks. Guess what? He did not like that asscrack sandpaper sensation one tiny bit. So halfway down the bike path we had to stop. I took off his underwear. I spread his little butt cheeks and tried to dislodge said sand from the crevice, using my bare hand. That's right: I'm credit-carding my naked kid in front of approximately twenty people. All I wanted in that moment was a pressure hose to appear from the skies, to clean off this sand and poop and also my dignity. We had another half mile to go.

Jafta got tired. He didn't want to ride his bike anymore. He started crying. Loudly. I started yelling. Loudly.

"KEEP GOING, JAFTA!"

He didn't want to keep going, so he started falling on purpose. Every time he fell, I chastised him. We were a weepy, poopy, sandy, wet, sunburned, mostly naked mess. People were staring. All I could think about was getting back to that car. For the next twenty minutes, I practically cattle-prodded a screaming Jafta while pushing a stroller with a screaming toddler while screaming at both of them myself. The grand finale was when I realized I had to put the poop-bike into the back of my car, the smell causing me to dry-heave the entire ride home.

I had become that mother I swore I would never be—the mom with a poop stain above her boobs. Except it was tiny flecks of poop in my hair and a biohazard bike in the back of the minivan I never wanted.

READY, SET, NOPE: HOW TO FAIL AT MOTHERHOOD BEFORE YOU EVEN START

Women often endure infertility, pregnancy, infant loss, miscarriages, and stillbirths in isolation, because while sadness is a socially palatable response to these often life-altering events, rage, frustration, jealousy, and guilt are not.

SORAYA CHEMALY

When you decide to have kids, you must kill the illusion that you have any control over outcomes. It is a dangerous fantasy that will break your heart. When your life is intrinsically tied to other human beings, you have two choices: (a) spend a lifetime worrying about every possible outcome for people who ultimately grow up to make their own decisions, or (b) surrender to the reality that life is full of beauty and hurt and we can't really control the incidence of either. I've spent a lot of time trying to move from *a* to *b*.

For some of us, that illusion of control started to fracture before the kids even came. There is no unpredictability quite like how you become a parent. From unplanned pregnancies to surprise C-sections to unexpected multiples, there are so many aspects of bringing a child into this world that happen outside of and despite our own agendas.

My husband and I had been trying to get pregnant for almost a year when I finally got that first positive pregnancy test. By that time, a lot of the sheen had worn off the process. The first month was all excitement and promise, and each time we had sex without barriers, it felt like this meaningful experience. *We might have just made a baby together.* I tried to commit each moment to my memory.

I fully expected to get pregnant that first month. Sure, I had heard statistics about it taking most people a few months. But we were on it! We had our eyes on the prize. The sperm just had to meet the egg, and science would do its thing.

One unsuccessful month passed, followed by another. Disappointment set in. As a type-A personality with a knack for catastrophizing, I was the Very Worst at waiting to become pregnant. I was taking pregnancy tests on the first day they could possibly be positive, and then every day thereafter, until my dreams were dashed by getting my period. I went through pregnancy tests like a Kardashian goes through mascara. I sometimes took more than one a day, because *maybe my pee was just diluted!* I became obsessed.

Several months in, the romantic notions of making a baby as we made love were replaced with a cold, biological ritual of determination. Sex became a chore and a duty. Our intimacy (if you could even call it that) was dictated by ovulation calendars and bedside thermometers. It was less about mutual pleasure and more about a means to an end. "Time for the old insert and squirt," a fellow infertile friend joked about sex during that period.

At this time in my life, control was a core value for me. Infertility is the total loss of control. It is one of those life situations where Trying Hard may not take you any closer to the prize. And it's a betrayal that originates in your own body. *You* won't do the thing that you want most. Up until that point, I drew my worth from being effective, responsible, and capable. While this may have looked like confidence on the exterior, it came from a place of deep shame. I did not have a sense of my own inherent value. I couldn't have articulated this at the time—I thought I was just ambitious and driven. And while those things were true, there was also a well of insecurity that fueled everything I did. Not being able to get pregnant brought that insecurity to the surface.

As the months wore on, the fear set in.

By month six, I had made an appointment with a fertility doctor—or an RE (reproductive endocrinologist), as I learned from the infertility message boards I was reading, late into the night, from my laptop, in the dark living room. I also began begging my husband to switch gears and pursue adoption. I had always wanted to adopt. But my husband, while seemingly game for adoption in the distant future, thought it made more sense to get pregnant first. He thought I was stressing out too much about it anyway. He figured it would happen for us sooner or later. My panic grew. At the same time, his commitment to *not* panic grew firmer.

And this was the unfortunate emotional cycle of our marriage: I catastrophized, he avoided and minimized. I blew things out of proportion, he detached. The result was that it left me feeling misunderstood, discounted, and alone, while he felt like I was creating crises and drama.

Both of us were right.

During this season my constant worry pushed against his desire to avoid discomfort at all costs, and the chasm between us grew. I became angry at his lack of empathy, his lack of emotional investment, and his avoidance. He became annoyed at my monthly emotional roller coaster and my inability to snap out of it. He withdrew, which made me speak louder for him to hear me, which made him withdraw more. Rinse and repeat.

As I was struggling with infertility, nearly every friend in my close circle became pregnant, many with their second child. I felt like all of our friends were moving into a totally different stage of life and I was being left behind. Nights out with friends now centered around mom-talk: breastfeeding woes, sleeping through the night, pregnancy ailments, preschool decisions. It felt like every outing with friends turned into a painful reminder that I was not a mother.

It was an alienating and lonely time. Occasionally I asked friends if we could have a night where we didn't talk about kids. This proved difficult for them as new motherhood was, naturally, all-consuming. They began to feel that they couldn't be themselves around me, and I could feel the distance growing.

This is part of the unspoken pain of infertility. No one means to drop you as a friend, but the statute of limitations on sadness and moping eventually runs out. People find you to be negative and brooding. They get tired of walking on eggshells as it pertains to pregnancy and babies. And you get tired of going to girls' nights out that involve several hours of triggering conversations and painful reminders that you are missing out. In retrospect, I wish I had given myself permission to opt out of more of those outings, and to let go of the guilt of missing a few baby showers.

Finally, about a year into trying, two lines appeared. I took a few minutes to relish the news alone before calling my husband. He was overjoyed, and we cried and laughed on the phone. It was finally happening for us. In the coming weeks I could think of nothing but the baby growing inside me. I felt grateful. I felt at peace. I felt like my world had finally clicked into the correct channel. I shopped for maternity clothes. I made gleeful announcements to the friends who were still tolerating me. I signed up for BabyCenter and marked my due date on my calendar.

My happiness lasted ten weeks before things went wrong. I was standing onstage at church, leading worship, when something started feeling particularly *not right*. As I sang the phrase "Through many dangers, toils and snares, I have already come . . ." I felt a strange cramping sensation.

Surely God would not let me have a miscarriage during the third verse of "Amazing Grace." *This will be a really messed up memory if I am having a miscarriage right now,* I remember thinking to myself. I finished the rest of the set, fighting back tears because my abdomen was tightening in a way that I knew wasn't good. Once we finished singing, the pastor prayed the parting prayer, and I could sneak off the stage. I beelined to the bathroom, where I found a streak of fresh blood on my underwear. I walked to my car in tears, and texted my husband to meet me in the parking lot, because I couldn't deal with seeing people.

Later that afternoon, there was more pain. What first felt like cramps became more acute. It was a deep, low pinching pain. I didn't realize it at the time, but my cervix had begun dilating and I was going into labor.

We headed to urgent care. By that point I was struggling to walk and blacking out a bit from the pain. They took me in pretty quickly, asking me to disrobe and sit on an exam table covered in butcher paper. As I sat down, the bleeding started. So much blood. A nurse came in and seemed horrified and vaguely annoyed, like I was the first person to bleed on this table. Being a codependent people-pleaser, I started apologizing profusely, and tried to clean up. She had me sit on what looked like a giant adult diaper and asked me to lie back down so she could try to find the baby's heartbeat with a Doppler. I remember watching her face, attempting to read the results in her expression. I knew what was happening before the words came out of her mouth.

There was no heartbeat.

A doctor arrived. He gave me a paper bag and a lab container. He told me to go home and wait for the fetal tissue to expel, then to collect it in the container and put it in the fridge so that I could return it for testing.

That morning, I had a baby. That afternoon, I had *fetal tissue.* Fetal tissue that I needed to collect and put in my fridge, next to the cream cheese and the salad dressing.

We drove home in shock. I was no longer pregnant but not entirely *not* pregnant. This aspect of miscarriage no one talks about. I'm not sure what I thought happened, but it never occurred to me that a miscarried baby must still be delivered. I had a dead "something" inside me. A fetus/baby/tissue that I had to expel. It felt morbid and gross, and I wanted it to be over. It was a strange feeling: wanting this awful thing to hurry up and be finished, but also not wanting it to happen at all.

We got home and I took some pain relievers and sat on the couch with a heating pad. A couple friends stopped by and brought me ice cream. They prayed with me. They prayed for a miracle. They fervently asked, in faith, for God to save my baby. I know they meant well, but their prayers made me angry. Praying for a miracle felt like setting me up for disappointment. I didn't want any more of that. As they prayed, I felt my neck get hot. I wanted to crawl out of my skin. *This prayer is bullshit,* I thought to myself. *My uterus is bleeding out into my underwear. We aren't getting a miracle.* I didn't want to participate in what felt like a charade, but I sat there because I didn't want to explain my theology. I just wanted them to leave.

For the next few hours I sat on my sofa in the saddest state of expectation I had ever experienced. I was also in some of the worst pain I've experienced, because I was essentially in labor. At one point, the pain intensified and I went to the bathroom. When I pulled down my underwear, I discovered the fetus/baby/tissue had passed. It fell from my underwear onto the floor of my bathroom and I looked at it in horror. This unformed, flesh-colored mass was the baby I had been waiting for all my life. I was disgusted that this plop onto the porcelain tile floor of my bathroom was the undignified entry for this long-anticipated baby. I called for my husband and put the tissue into the doctor-provided canister. Then I put my baby into a brown bag and into my fridge. That was when the reality of it consumed me. I lay on my bed and sobbed. And I stayed there for the better part of a week.

If my friends were struggling to understand how to support me through my infertility, this became even more difficult after the miscarriage. I was distraught. I vacillated between desperately wanting to talk about what I was going through and not wanting to talk about it at all. It was unpredictable, and it left the people in my life tiptoeing around me. I understood how I was pushing people away. But I couldn't get outside of my own feelings and grief.

I experienced another year of infertility after my miscarriage before getting pregnant again. I was equally relieved and excited and afraid to get my hopes up. When I miscarried a few weeks later, the same devastating cycle kicked back into gear. When you are a person already prone to anxiety, having your worst fears realized confirms all those negative thoughts. They're fuel to an already lit match, the irrational belief that if you worry in advance about every possible outcome it will lessen the blow if something bad happens again.

At this point, my friends were providing well-intentioned but hurtful advice. *Maybe you need to relax more. Maybe you're trying to control the situation too much. Maybe if you just distract yourself with other things it will finally happen.* Everyone seemed to think they knew more than medical science, I was bad at pregnancy, apparently, because I worried too much.

After my second miscarriage, my doctor told me it was still highly likely that my next pregnancy would be normal. "We don't panic unless you've had three in a row," he said in an effort to comfort me.

My birthday that year began with another miscarriage. It was my third in a row in two years of trying to get pregnant.

That was when I really did panic. I knew the statistics. I was starting to feel hopeless and helpless. My body was betraying me. It kept expelling, over and over, the thing I wanted to keep the most.

I started to wonder if God was punishing me. I don't believe in a punitive God. I had already abandoned the notion of a cruel and vengeful God I'd learned about in my evangelical upbringing. But when you are in the midst of trauma and pain, your brain tries to make connections, regardless of how irrational they might be. Your mind tries to process cause and effect, linking point A to point B. I started to wonder if this was happening for a reason. Was it because we hadn't pursued adoption first? Maybe my desire to adopt was a *calling.* (Which can be a fancy Christianese term for "something that God tells you to do that you'd better not ignore" or also "something you feel like doing but you don't want to explain yourself so you designate it a *call-*

ing.") Maybe I was being disobedient. Selfish. Biologically ego-centric. Or maybe I just didn't have enough faith.

That thought was fueled by the advice of many well-meaning friends. "Kristen, you've really just got to trust God on this" was a frequent response when I shared how scared, sad, and hope-less I felt. "You're just gonna have to have faith on this one," my friends would admonish me.

But what is the subtext in that statement? Why do we tell people going through horrible circumstances to "just have faith"? It's terrible theology. It implies that our faith can guide outcomes. And yet, in my desperation, I began to buy it. During some of my miscarriages, at the first sign of bleeding, I would lie prostrate on the floor, crying out to God, making promises to trust Him, proclaiming that I had the faith that He could heal me. And when He didn't, it crushed me. In those moments, I truly believed I could will God into miraculous action by the fervency of my faith.

Christians don't like to sit with the idea that, sometimes, God doesn't save us from our pain. And when that inevitably happens—because pain and suffering are part of the human experience—we have a crisis of faith.

After miscarriage three, I announced that God and I were "on a break." When friends tried to offer the expected Christian platitudes, I started to push back. I became surly, challenging both their theology and their empathy skills. "Why can't you just sit with me in my pain?" I started asking. "Why do you feel the need to implore me to have more faith? I *had* faith. It didn't change anything."

Here is the sticky thing about Christians and pain: Tragedy and suffering are bad press. If you didn't grow up in Christian circles, here is a peek backstage: We love a good redemption story but we hate the messy middle. We want the story to come to a redemptive conclusion. We want to wrap it up in a pretty bow. Sure, you might have been in pain *but then Jesus.* We want to point to the place where God pulled us out of our pain, but when we can't find our way out of it, the narrative doesn't work. Why won't God save us from suffering? (For what it's worth, this narrative around God saving us from suffering isn't something the Bible promises. Nonetheless, we believe it.)

At the time, my husband was working as a youth pastor, so we were pretty entrenched in Christian circles. I remember at one point, his boss—our senior pastor—called my husband aside and told him that there was some concern among the elder board about how I was "handling my miscarriages." I guess me not bouncing back was making them uncomfortable. I'm not sure how this had any bearing on Mark's job, but it was implied: *Get your wife in order. Her grief is too loud.*

And then I had miscarriage number four. This was when I got called into my doctor's office for The Talk.

MIRACLE BABY

All that we love deeply becomes a part of us.

HELEN KELLER

My fertility doctor's name was Dr. Werlin, and he looked like a cross between Mick Jagger and Albert Einstein. He had shocking white hair that hit his shoulders and seemed to add three inches to his head on all sides. His entire office was a tribute to his love of the Rolling Stones. The walls were covered floor-to-ceiling in Rolling Stones memorabilia. There were signed records and photos of Dr. Werlin with the band, but there were also photos of pregnant women in Rolling Stones shirts, of babies in various poses from album scenes, and patient-submitted artwork. It was odd, but also strangely soothing. Quirky and disarming are welcome distractions in an office where so much serious stuff happens. I mean, how can you panic during an ultrasound when "Satisfaction" is blaring?

The exam rooms at Dr. Werlin's office were *always* playing the Rolling Stones. And yet somehow, when bad news was delivered, the volume subtly and ceremoniously turned down. You might have been listening to "Brown Sugar" as Dr. Werlin squirted your stomach with lube or put the condom on the transvaginal ultrasound. But a nurse would quietly turn down Keith Richards's blaring guitar when it became obvious there was no heartbeat and hard news had to be delivered. I'd had the Rolling Stones turned down on me a time or two.

After my fourth miscarriage and a battery of new tests to figure out why, I got a call from Dr. Werlin's office. "The doctor would like to have you come in to discuss things in person."

This is never a call you want from a doctor, because it means bad news. Good news can be left in a voicemail. Good news can be delivered by a nurse over the phone. A doctor's office is like middle school. When you get called into the office, shit is about to get real. I made the earliest appointment they had available, which was a week away. Which meant I had to deal with the stress of ambiguity for a full week. Don't doctors know this is torture?

For seven days I pretended to be a normal, functioning person, when inside my head I was writing and rewriting a Lifetime movie script about my sad doctor's appointment. What he would say. What it all meant. How brave I would be. How brave I would not be. I was a ball of anxiety and could think of nothing else.

But deep down I knew.

And on that afternoon a week after our fourth miscarriage, when we had our somber meeting with Dr. Werlin, there was no music. In fact, there were no patients at all. In the mornings, the infertiles and the pregnants shared a space in Dr. Werlin's waiting room. It instilled hope to see so many happy successfully pregnant patients in the practice. But in the afternoon, the place became quiet and somber. This was the time for hard conversations. You did not want to be an afternoon patient, because it meant things weren't looking promising in the baby department.

Sitting down in his office, I didn't feel nervous, I felt sad. I already had a pretty good pulse on what Dr. Werlin was going to tell us. Like most people I had already diagnosed myself with the help of Google. I shouldn't have been surprised.

But still, it was shocking to hear the words come out of his mouth that indicated we had come to the end of the end. His livelihood, after all, was creating "miracle babies" through the advancement of reproductive technology. And according to the myriad of baby pictures on his walls and the brand-new Porsche he had parked outside, he was good at it.

Dr. Werlin had no definitive explanation for our recurrent pregnancy loss. He mentioned some high-tech treatment options but explained that while IVF could help me get pregnant, it could not help me *stay* pregnant. I joked that IVF sounded like an expensive way for me to have another miscarriage, and he didn't disagree. I told him I thought we were done with treatments. He did not push us, and when he suggested a referral to an adoption agency, I let him know that I was already on it.

In the previous month, despite being pregnant, I had put an application in to the foster-adopt program with our local Department of Children and Family Services. This was the first decision in building a family that I felt truly at peace about.

I wanted to be a mother more than I wanted to be pregnant. Dr. Werlin's news was a swerve in that path, but I was already walking that curve. I had always wanted to adopt, and once I started having an ominous feeling about the fate of number four, adoption became my resolve. Dr. Werlin's words could have felt like a life sentence. Instead, they felt like a relief. We could stop trying. *A fertility doctor* gave me permission to stop trying. And I no longer had to convince my husband. While he didn't heed *my* petitions to get off this crazy train, he did hear the words from the professional. After meeting with Dr. Werlin, my husband and I agreed to put our energy into the adoption process. We started attending classes to become certified as foster parents.

The first step in adoption is completing a homestudy. A homestudy involves an inspection of your home, as well as every corner of your personal life. It's basically an audition to be a parent. They ask you questions about your relationship, your family of origin, your abuse history, your sex life. No question is too invasive. Your private life is laid bare as a social worker decides whether or not you are fit to be a parent.

This is especially demoralizing when you consider that none of your friends had to "get approval" to have a baby. None of the other mothers I knew had to hang a fire extinguisher in their kitchen, buy a safe for their medications, or put child-safety locks on literally every cabinet of the house.

Another unnerving aspect of the homestudy is the checklist you have to fill out to indicate what kind of child you are willing to accept. Will you take a child with a physical deformity? A medical condition? Cognitive delays? What race are you open to? Will you take siblings? What ages are you willing to accept? Filling out this checklist felt like a measure of my humanity. I felt like, if I was truly unselfish, I would check yes on every single box. What kind of a person says no to a child with a disability? No to a cleft palate? What are you, a *monster*? These are questions most parents will never be asked. When you give birth to a child with a disability you deal with the hand you are dealt. When you get a checklist, you have to make some brutal decisions that make you feel like an asshole.

As I researched more about adoption I came to understand something my friend and fellow adoption parent Claudia Chapman refers to as The Queue. There is a queue on both sides of the adoption process. There is a line of waiting parents, and there is a line of waiting children. Unfortunately, these lines do not often meet because the parents are waiting for a specific kind of child: typically white, newborn, and perfectly healthy. On the other side of the queue, the children waiting for parents tend to be older, children of color, often with siblings, difficult backgrounds, or medical needs.

It was really important to me that I adopt a child that really needed a family. I did not want to be another couple in line for the perfect healthy white newborn. I wanted to be a family for a child who might not otherwise find one. This was why we decided to adopt from foster care. I knew that black children were overrepresented in that queue. Both of my sisters had multiracial kids. So I was very open to a child of color.

A few weeks after being certified, we got a call from our social worker. It was about a baby boy. He was African American, six months old, and living with an elderly foster mother that was not a permanent placement. Did we want to meet him?

I was incredibly nervous for this meeting. Could this be the day we meet our son? I felt tension between wanting to find meaning in the moment and being too traumatized from past losses to trust anything. I was the woman who had tried to remember something distinct about each time we had sex while trying to get pregnant. I steeled myself, and tried to be rational and stoic, but it didn't work. I was a ball of emotion.

We arrived at the Department of Children and Family Services in Compton and were led into a sterile, fluorescent-lit office. The foster mom was running late, so we made small talk with the social worker while I tried to swallow my panic. Finally, they arrived. The baby was taken from his foster mom in another office by a social worker, and then ushered into our room and plopped into our arms as the social worker made a hasty exit.

And this baby was understandably not happy about it.

The social worker told us she would give us some time to "get to know each other," which sounds perfectly appropriate until you realize half of the equation is a scared six-month-old who is pissed he just got handed to strangers. There were absolutely no toys or anything else of interest to a child in the room and I remember being annoyed by that, but then simultaneously disappointed that I hadn't had the foresight to bring something for him to play with. I was failing already.

The little boy continued to cry. He was really distressed. Nothing we did could console him. This meeting was going badly. I didn't feel a spark, or a wash of emotion. Mostly I felt tired and nervous at this crying baby. Where did that social worker go? Why didn't she come back in? How long do we have to sit here with this screaming infant? Is this not the kid for us? As I grappled with the desire to be rescued, a new wave of insecurity hit me. How am I supposed to be his mom if I can't even soothe this kid for twenty minutes? Is this what motherhood is like? I wondered what it would be like living with this inconsolable child in my living room.

I tried to stare at him and get some sign from God. He was cute, undoubtedly cute. He had rubbed a patch of hair off the back of his head, which gave the impression of a bald smile above his neck. He was dressed in plaid overalls and an orange polo shirt embroidered with a teddy bear—an outfit I would never choose. I searched his face for some sign of recognition or confirmation. Is this my son? He just kept crying.

Finally the social worker came back in. I tried to act unfazed. I didn't want her to register my panic, or my relief at her return. I made jokes, acted casual. *Whatevs, he's kinda screamy, NBD.*

She told us to go home and think about it and call her tomorrow.

The drive home felt heavy, because I really wasn't sure. I felt defeated and demoralized by not feeling sure. My husband felt the same way. We shrugged our shoulders. We wondered aloud if he always cried that much. We rationalized that surely, in our own house, consoling him would be easier. We admitted he was pretty cute. But neither of us had a strong conviction.

I thought meeting my child would be the stuff of movies. A blinding, searing moment of recognition and love. I thought there would be a swell of emotion. I didn't imagine sitting scared and nervous in an empty office on ripped vinyl chairs, hoping someone would come and relieve me. I expected to be struck by certainty. Certainty didn't come.

Still, we said yes.

We said yes and in four days, we were scheduled to take custody of our son. Just like that. For four years we had tried to become parents, and in four days, it happened.

I didn't feel relief. Not yet. I mostly felt nervous and numb. Like I was watching a movie of my life. I spent four days in a flurry of shopping and planning and decorating, giving this kid the nursery of dreams. Or at least of a Land of Nod catalog.

On placement day, my husband and I woke up early, installed a brand-new car seat, and drove to the Department of Children and Family Services once again. We nervously buckled a six-month-old little boy named Jafta into our car, and drove him home, stealing glances at him the whole way.

The first day was surreal. I feel like I actually met my son once he was home. His expression of stress and confusion melted away, and he started having fun. As it turns out, he had quite a personality. He was LOUD. He loved to laugh. He was a bruiser, he liked getting into things and was trying his best to crawl. We set him in a bouncy seat and he squealed and laughed and bid for our attention. He was, by all counts, a very typical six-month-old with a big personality, and I felt my doubt begin to subside.

That night, I rocked him to sleep, and stared into his eyes as he drank from a bottle. As I held him, I felt washed by a surge of love I'd never experienced in my life. For the first time, I felt like a mother.

A few months after Jafta joined our family, I got an invitation from Dr. Werlin to come to his infertility practice's annual "Miracle Baby" party. I'd known about this annual celebration for his patients who had found success at having a baby (or in many cases, thanks to IVF, two or three at a time).

Over the years, I was skeptical about this term. Is it really a "miracle baby" if you paid $40k and underwent three medical procedures to have it? Isn't that kind of the opposite of a miracle? Wouldn't it be more accurate if it was called a "Thank God for Modern Science" party? Or "My Parents Went into Massive Debt to Have Me" party? Nonetheless, I was touched that Dr. Werlin included us after having received our adoption announcement and I decided that I would go to the Miracle Baby party.

We dressed Jafta in his cutest outfit and set out for the park location, clearly the oddball couple with an obviously adopted child at an event for children created with the assistance of reproductive technology. We stood in the line to get a picture with Dr. Werlin and after he met Jafta, he hugged me and congratulated me. Our family photo hangs on the gallery wall along with all of the other miracle babies from his practice. His inclusion was a small gesture, but it meant a lot.

For me, the anguish and pain and anxiety of those years of infertility and miscarriage finally began to heal as I fell in love with Jafta, my miracle baby through adoption.

I thought that nature would be what made me a mother. But in reality, it was nurture that made me a mother. Nurturing my son allowed me to affirm my own role as a mom, regardless of how I got there. I was able to lean into motherhood as a verb, not as a place to arrive.

I "HAD IT ALL," RIGHT ON THE FRONT OF MY SHIRT

Of course I'm not supposed to admit that there is triannual torrential sobbing in my office, because it's bad for the feminist cause. It makes it harder for women to be taken seriously in the workplace. It makes it harder for other working moms to justify their choice. But I have friends who stay home with their kids and they also have a triannual sob, so I think we should call it even. I think we should be kind to one another about it. I think we should agree to blame the children.

TINA FEY

I went back to work pretty quickly after adopting my first child. At the time, I worked part-time as a marriage and family therapist, and part-time as an adjunct professor in the grad psych department at a local university. Work was a welcome change to life with an infant. I enjoyed getting out of the house, getting dressed in grown-up clothes, and being around other adults. My job provided me with a nice jolt of intellectual stimulation to break up the monotony inherent in being a mom. I felt good. Prideful, even. I am having it all! This isn't so hard?

About a year later, I would go on to have an unexpected, surprising, healthy, full-term pregnancy that ended with a baby.

(More on that emotional and amazing and terrifying experience later.)

Baby #2 slept about two hours at a time. She nursed 24/7. I was tired all the time. I was plagued with postpartum anxiety that made me even more of a catastrophizer than I already am. I no longer felt like getting dressed and going to work was a nice reprieve. Now it felt like a complete and total charade. I was a stressed sleepwalker in a professional pantsuit. Underneath my blazer was a bulky maternity bra and leaky boobs. I struggled to stay awake as my clients talked about their lives. I showed up to class with spit-up stains on my shirt.

A few years later I carried a baby to term again. Once I had my third child, my brain was in short-circuit mode. I just couldn't get my head into a space where I could be present with clients. Motherhood was draining all of the energy I had previously devoted to my job.

Then we adopted a fourth child and I hit rock bottom.

I knew I wasn't functioning well. Splitting parenting shifts with a spouse sounds like a great idea, until you realize it means you are never "off." We didn't have help, it was just me, being a full-time mom any second of the day I wasn't working, often doing both at the same time, and feeling like something had to give.

It seemed like every night I was scheduled to teach, there was some crisis getting out of the door. One evening, I was scrambling and shoving papers into my laptop bag. It had been raining quite a bit in the previous few days and I had noticed a trail of ants leading from the front door into the kitchen earlier in the day. I knew I should deal with it, but as happens with a houseful of children, I got distracted and forgot.

I threw my work outfit on as soon as my husband came home, running out while weaving around small, dirty children seeking to soil my clothes. Kind of like *The Walking Dead,* only instead of escaping zombies, I was avoiding children with outstretched hands covered in peanut butter or tempera paint. I made it to the car without incident. I threw my bag into the seat next to me and headed to campus.

When I arrived, I slung my bag over my shoulder and started the hike to class, with the smug feeling of a woman who is *doing this thing.*

You know. The feeling of a mom with combed hair and a dry-cleaned outfit. The mom who has a thriving work/kids/self-care balance.

Halfway to class I started feeling a little heebie-jeebie. A little creepy-crawly. I suddenly realized a literal army of disoriented ants was crawling all over me. They had descended upon an errant Goldfish cracker that made its way into my bag over the weekend. They had feasted in the warm recesses of a front pocket in the comfort of my kitchen, and then they proceeded to disperse all over my body on the grassy knoll between Parking Lot C and Heath Academic Center.

There were ants on my arms, in my hair, everywhere. But I had a class waiting for me, and that bag needed to come with me. That bag held the laptop that stored the PowerPoint presentation that was my only hope of forming a coherent thought in front of thirty-seven graduate students.

I upended the bag and removed the offensive piece of food, but the ants were still all over me.

I had no choice but to continue walking to class, wiping ants from my body and shaking my arms and legs the entire way. I arrived a little late and I had to start right into my lecture, all the while pinching and flinging ants from my clothing as my students looked on in horror.

Had I been teaching my addiction class, I could have weaved

this into a lecture on the effects of crystal meth. Instead, it just served as a lesson in humility. And a hit to my pride.

Professor Howerton before kids was fun and youthful and put-together. She showed up early and dressed well. She was energetic and spicy.

Professor Howerton after kids showed up harried and disheveled. She was late and flustered and seemed distracted. She showed up with ants in her clothes and milk on her shirt. She was going through the motions. She mostly just wanted to go home.

I didn't like this version of myself. I take a lot of pride in doing things well, and I did not feel like I was doing well at work. It's not like I was nailing it at home, either.

On paper, my schedule worked. But there is a daily cavalcade of unplanned crises that comes with having multiple little kids. That crisis could come in the form of a diaper blowout, or deciding to make an art project with the Scantron forms you need for your students that night, or a call from the school that there's been a lice outbreak. Or a kid getting the flu. Or pinkeye. Or a dentist appointment that results in a filling that results in a child gnawing the skin off her lip while numb from novocaine that becomes infected that results in another doctor's appointment. Having kids is like one big episode of *If You Give a Mouse a Cookie*, only with child-related catastrophes.

All of these unforeseen things were pushing on the narrow margins I'd allotted myself for working. I felt like a bystander, watching my time get sucked away by minutiae, and my windows of productive activity grow smaller and smaller. Pretty much every day I would concede, "Well, I guess I'll finish my to-do list at midnight after I deal with today's surprise chaos."

I loved being a mom, and I loved being a mom with a career, but I couldn't help feeling like somewhere along the line I'd been sold a bill of goods that anyone could really pull off both. I was working nonstop, forgoing sleep, and wondering what would crop up to keep me from finishing the projects for deadlines I needed to make yesterday.

But I wanted to *have it all,* dammit. Even though it was feeling, increasingly, like *having it all* was making me crazy. I was desperate for a solution to the stress I was living under.

We finally decided to try hiring a nanny for two days a week, so that my husband and I could work on the same days and not feel like we were pulling split-shifts. But we discovered that finding someone to care for four kids five and under was not an easy task. The first woman I hired was amazing when playing with the kids. They had a blast together. But I would come home from work and spend my evening cleaning up from the day, doing laundry, unloading the dishwasher. I still was doing the difficult aspects of being a stay-at-home mom while working outside of the home. She was a college student and ended up going home for the summer, so I was more explicit with the next person I hired about the scope of the job. "You've got to do everything I would do if I was at home," I tried to explain. I walked her through how I kept the wheels on. Clean up while they watch a show. Move the laundry forward while they take a nap. Sweep up while they play. This gal lasted about a month before she let me know she was moving on to a family with two older kids. I can't say I blamed her.

I don't think my kids were uniquely difficult, there are just a lot of them, closely spaced. We burned through three nannies in six months. The last nanny who left mentioned her concerns about the fact that after she worked so hard to clean and organize, everything would be back to its messy state within a few days. She felt frustrated that she had to spend so much time feeding and cleaning up after the kids that it took away from time just relaxing and having fun with them. Um, wel-come to my world. THOSE ARE THE THINGS WE HIRED YOU TO DO.

Yet I also understood exactly where she was coming from. *YES. Those things suck. I wouldn't want to work at a place where those things were my job. I often feel trapped by these responsi-bilities, as well.* I remember laughing with a friend as I recounted this story. "I can't even *pay* someone to do my life. Not even for two days a week!" It was funny, but also sobering.

Eventually, I did decide to leave the workforce. I could not figure out how to balance being a mother with taking care of clients and students who were depending on me, too. My hus-band and I were trying to split-shift work and parenting and it was stressful for both of us. We decided he would increase his work hours, we would tighten the belt financially, and I would focus on the kids. I'd love to report that my issues magically re-solved when I no longer had work to contend with. In truth, I missed the purpose and identity of having a job. While the re-sponsibilities of a career were overwhelming with four kids, I still liked the idea and the optics of it. I missed getting dressed and using multisyllabic words and having a title.

I found the monotony of full-time motherhood to be mind-numbingly boring. I know there are mothers for whom this isn't true, and I raise a glass to them, because it isn't me. I like the affirmation of a job well done. And that doesn't happen at home with kids. It's just a cycle of tasks that have to be repeated the very next day. Every day was Groundhog Day. Wake up (too early). Get everyone fed. Clean up the breakfast mess. Make lunches. Clean up the lunch mess. Put them down for naps. Do some laundry. Panic when they wake up too early. Make dinner. Clean up. Give baths. Read stories. Fight to get them to sleep. The laundry basket I cleared today would be full tomorrow. The clean table would be covered in crumbs tomorrow. The old cliché is that a woman's work is never done, but I was finding the cycles were driving me insane.

You cannot measure a mother's love for her children . . . and I found this fact difficult. I was working hard to love them well, but those tasks felt so unquantifiable. I liked gold stars and performance reviews and report cards. I like having some external measure that I'm doing a good job, but everything I was doing to love my children well was repetitive and unseen.

From an early age women have been socialized to look for external validation and that doesn't end when we have children. My whole life, I had looked for accolades to tell me I was enough. I had to make a conscious choice, every single day, to just "be" with my kids. Just reading this book to them. Just singing this lullaby. Just lying here and cuddling. These things were thankless, and they were immeasurable. But they were the work of motherhood in those years. Not being a supermom, but being a mom who was present in the moments that matter.

It's unfortunate that the decision to work, or not work, is one that has left mothers feeling guilt. Whether it was out of boredom or a desire for connection or an unhealthy need to be affirmed for the job I was doing, I started blogging more once I left the workforce. Within a few years blogging morphed from a hobby into a full-time work-from-home job. I went from being a working mom to a stay-at-home mom to a work-at-home mom, and I am here to report: It's all hard. Each option has pros and cons, and the decision is entirely personal and entirely dependent on kids, ages, temperament, personality, finances, spousal contribution, and a whole host of other factors specific to each mom.

I don't think this is usually an overt "mommy war" and I think (hope) it's a rare occurrence, but I have definitely felt shamed in my tenure as a mother for working. I can remember once being at a school function and overhearing two moms smugly observing that they were there at least once a week when most of us could only show up for the "big stuff" at the holidays. Why, yes. That was absolutely true. Because a lot of us had jobs, and there is nothing in the parenting handbook that says that mothers must demonstrate their love to their children by volunteering at their school at least once a week. No child is going to therapy over that.

In fact, I will say that in the decade I worked as a therapist, I never had a client traumatized over having a working mom, or over having a stay-at-home mom. Barring being totally neglected by a caregiver, this is a nonissue. Kids absolutely need love and attention and affection. They need consistency and responsiveness. But this can be provided by a mom who works, with the help of a caring nanny or childcare center or relative or (gasp) stay-at-home father. I mean, they do need *someone* there caring for them until they are of a certain age . . . we can all agree on that, right? But as long as that babysitter/grandparent/daycare provider/father is loving and attentive, the kids will be all right if Mom goes to work.

I have noticed that help is another shame point with moms. I know countless mothers who have regular help, be it while they work at an office or from their home or not at all, and are really reticent to talk about their nanny. There is no shame in having hired help. I was never able to make it work for myself, but it was not for lack of trying. I know that the nanny shaming is real, because I've heard other mothers do it. "Oh, she has help," they say, in a tone that could also be used for, "Oh, she kills puppies."

"Must be nice to have a nanny do the hard stuff while you run off to work every day."

Side note: Can we retire the phrase "must be nice"? First of all, it is almost entirely used to passive-aggressively cut another person down. Second of all, most of the time, it's an arbitrary comment on someone's life choices that just happen to be different than yours. Yes, it "must be nice" to not have to get up and go to work every morning, but it also "must be nice" to be able to leave the house. We can take this phrase and basically heap shame on every person in every situation that isn't our own, and it's dumb.

Feminism gave us the gift of being able to choose, but if we are not careful, having the freedom to do *anything* can easily morph into the obligation to do *everything*—and that's a recipe for exhaustion and despair, not liberation. An inherent aspect of choice is choosing one thing over another. By learning to say no to certain roles or obligations of motherhood that don't work for us, we allow ourselves to more fully embrace the roles that we actively choose for ourselves. Not the roles our parents or society or even our spouses hoist upon us but the ones that resonate from our unique personalities and passions. Even if that looks like doing less. Even if it means no gold stars.

Ultimately we are all fighting the same battle. Working mom or stay-at-home mom, one truth remains: Every mom, on some level, has to assume that 50 percent of her day will be spent doing something she didn't plan for and probably won't remember later.

GIVE ME DOWNTIME OR GIVE ME DEATH

I really love my kids for about six minutes a day.

MICHAEL IAN BLACK

One day, when my little ones were really small, I was chatting with my sister-in-law about being a mom. She had her two babies around the same time I did. She was talking about how much she loved her kids. When they were napping, she would go in and watch them sleep. "Don't you just feel like you can't wait for them to wake up?" she asked. "Sometimes I'm tempted to wake them up just so I can cuddle and play with them."

I tried to hold a neutral expression of understanding, but inside, I was thinking, *HELL NO*. I had never, in my few years as a parent, wanted to wake a sleeping child. Her words were confusing but also punched me in the gut a bit. I felt the exact opposite. After a couple hours of wrangling and feeding and changing diapers and answering questions, I couldn't wait for them to nap and I was usually mildly irritated when they woke up. I felt the same way about bedtime. After dinner, I was basically counting down the hours until I could put them to sleep. When they finally went down, I was like Gollum with his ring. The solitude was My Precious. Why did my sister-in-law feel so differently? Did she have some innate mothering instinct that I lacked?

In those early years with four kids under four, I was overwhelmed and outnumbered. The volume of work it took to keep my household running was exhausting. But there was something more draining than physical fatigue: Parenting was emotionally exhausting. I tried hard to be a present mom who offered a listening ear, empathy, and unconditional love. But in reality, most of the time I just wanted to be alone. I felt trapped. I was longing for the days when no one needed me. I missed my pre-mom life where I could make an agenda and do the things I wanted to do, even if that involved sitting in the quiet of my own thoughts.

My overwhelming thoughts when they were sleeping were, *Please don't wake up. Please give me a little more time to myself. Please, just a few more minutes.* I couldn't imagine waking them up on purpose unless there was a fire.

I grew increasingly selfish about my alone time. If one of my kids started to fall asleep in the car or in the stroller on an errand, I would intentionally keep them awake so that they would sleep later, at home, and afford me some quiet headspace. What good was a sleeping baby in a grocery store? I needed the baby sleeping at my house, while my feet were up. I would watch one of their eyes start to droop in public and I would begin the pro-

cess of maniacally keeping them from sleeping. Singing songs?
I can do that. A silly dance? Sure. Right here in aisle 3. Anything
to keep them awake.

Nothing was more important than *my* nap time. I can remember one Thanksgiving when my mother was trying to plan
the day, and her proposed timeline meant that the kids would
miss napping. I asked if we could shift mealtime to a little later.
Couldn't everyone just plan their holiday around my two-year-
old? We got into an argument about it, and she accused me of
being inflexible. And the truth is, I was. My mom thought I was
being obsessive about their sleep schedule. But what she didn't
realize was that it was really about my own need for quiet. It felt
like I would decompose without it.

I started to feel shame about my desire to escape from my
own kids. Society* tells us that we should savor every precious
moment with our kids, and I was struggling to do this. If motherhood had been one of my biggest goals in life, why did I want to
get away from my children? Why did every day feel like a count-
down toward some relief from them? Maybe I was a horrible
mother. Or I suffered from some kind of defect, an intimacy
disorder, or psychological baggage that kept me from being able
to enjoy my children as much as other people did.

Because I was raised a good Christian girl and guilt is what
we do best, I created fatalistic narratives in my head. Maybe I
couldn't get pregnant for so long because God knew I would be
a shitty mom. Look how ungrateful I am for the gifts God gave.
I prayed for kids and now I just want a break from them.

Finally, the self-condemnation over this got to me enough
that I decided I needed to see a therapist. I made an appointment with a total stranger who had good reviews on Yelp,
walked into her office, and beelined for the tissues as I unloaded

---

* And by "society," I mean the Internet.

my horrible feelings about motherhood. I love my kids dearly, I told her. I enjoy being with them, in small doses. But I always felt like I needed a bigger chunk of time to myself. Like, if I could just spend three or four hours a day with them, life would be perfect. After that, I'm toast.

I was eager for the therapist to explain my glitch. Was I innately selfish? Was I a narcissist? I cried big, existential tears as I described my secret thoughts. After a few weeks of listening, my therapist pulled off her glasses and took the clipboard that usually sat on her lap and set it aside. She leaned in and asked me to listen closely to what she was going to say. She gave me a look like shit was about to get real. Pay attention.

"Kristen, you're an introvert," she said. "There is nothing wrong with you beyond the fact that you need time to yourself to refuel and recharge. You are running on empty. And you need to stop beating yourself up over the fact that you need time alone. It's how you're wired."

I'd never considered myself an introvert. I'm not shy. In fact, I can be pretty bold at times. I'm not scared to speak to a gathering of people or to command a room if I have something to say. I can be a leader. Some friends might even call me bossy. I like going to parties and socializing. I've always been the organizer and the connector in my social circle. If you put me in the middle of a group project, I will probably be the one delegating, taking notes, and leading the conversation.

I always assumed those traits meant I was an extrovert. But as my therapist explained to me, it's not about how I function in a crowd, but about what I need in order to refuel. I do like going to parties. But the next day, I'm usually exhausted and don't want to see other people. I've always struggled with all-day events. After a few hours, I'm itching to go home and I retreat into myself. I married into a family of extroverts who liked to do extended family events and invariably, about five hours in, one of them would pull my husband aside and ask if I was okay. And I was . . . kind of? But I guess five hours is the maximum time I can force myself to pretend to be extroverted, and after that I would sort of retreat into myself.

I also remember something a close friend had said to me before I had kids. She was a new mom and once mentioned, in an offhand way, that she didn't know how I would be able to parent "with all of the private time you require." Those words stung at the time. What was she talking about? But she saw me more accurately than I saw myself. I have always needed a lot of time to myself.

The more I thought about it with this new lens, the clearer it became. I'm not a bad mother; *I'm an introvert.*

I do not have to pine to be in my children's presence in order to love them. I do not have to spend every waking hour locked in a loving embrace to have a mama-bear love for my kids. Cars don't run on empty gas tanks, phones don't work on zero battery, and humans aren't as loving as we can be if we don't refuel and recharge. Love does not hinge on wanting to be around someone else 24/7. Anyone who has been married knows that's true.

I learned to take the advice I was constantly doling out to my own kids: Feelings and behaviors are two different things. It's okay if I sometimes feel sick of my kids. It's not okay if I act like it.

To any fellow introverts in the trenches of parenting young children, let me tell you the number one thing that helped me reconcile my introversion with parenting: They went off to school.

School is the number one thing that has improved my parenting. I've seen many a parent wax emotional on their child's first day of school, wishing they had more time in the nest and wondering how it happened so fast. Not me. I was dropping them off with glee, feeling like I just made it across the finish line of a marathon, high-fiving my fellow introverted mom friends. Children going to school for seven hours a day is a beautiful thing. God bless the teachers who deal with our children all day so we can get a break from them to do things like think or work or sit in silence.

With my kids in school, I finally had that experience my sister-in-law described . . . of looking forward to seeing my kids. I pick them up from school at three and I am legitimately excited to see them. When people ask me if I would ever homeschool I just laugh. Having my children go to school is the biggest tool in my parenting toolbox.

#ASSHOLEPARENT

So to you other kids all across the land
Take it from me, parents just don't understand

DJ JAZZY JEFF & THE FRESH PRINCE

For a good chunk of your tenure as a parent, your children probably won't like you.

This realization hit me as I was setting out a lunch for my youngest daughter when she was about four years old. Her older siblings were off at school, and it was just the two of us. To make the moment special I asked if she wanted to wear a princess gown to lunch and invite some of her stuffed animals. She seemed excited and hurried off to grab her collection of furry friends. I cut her sandwich into a fun puzzle shape with a new device I'd gotten. I blended a purple smoothie with her favorite frozen fruits. I cut grapes into quarters, and then carrots, exactly how she liked them. I served her food on a pretty pink plate, along with a matching pink cup.

As I sat down for lunch with her, my adorable daughter, wearing a tiara and a Disney Princess costume that cost more than most of my clothing, burst into tears. She laid her head down on the table and wailed. That was not an ample expression of her disappointment, so she lay down on the floor to continue the wailing. I stood there, dumbfounded. How did *any* of the things I just did lead to tears?

Well, I'll tell you how. I put a yellow straw into a pink cup. Like an asshole. I ruined her lunch, and she was very disappointed in me as a mother because of it. And I remember musing to myself, *It literally does not matter what I do for these kids. They are* always *disappointed in me.*

In that moment, with my daughter crying over a perfect lunch with a yellow straw, my instinct was to feel unappreciated. Defeated. I hovered there for a second.

Then I decided, I've got to find the humor here. I stealthily snapped a photo of her meltdown, described the scenario on Instagram, and tagged it #assholeparent.

Over the next few months I posted a few more sneak photos of meltdowns after I had been an awful mom. For example, when I gave her new shoes that were missing a light-up feature, or a burrito that had a tiny piece of cilantro on it. Soon I noticed that other parents were using the hashtag to document their own absurd stories, and I decided to curate them into an Instagram account that I aptly named @assholeparents. Within a month, that account had close to a million followers, with hundreds of parents posting their own #assholeparent moments every day.

It turns out this phenomenon is universal. Kids all around the world get frustrated when their parents try to ensure their safety or feed them.

In case you are wondering if you are an asshole parent, here are some questions to ask yourself. Have you ever given your child a broken granola bar or cookie and expected them to eat it? Have you ever asked your child to take a bath when they didn't want to take a bath? Have you ever taken your child to the grocery store after school instead of going straight home? Have you ever asked your child to eat foods that touch? Have you ever taken a teenager on a family vacation? If so, you might be an asshole parent.

Of course, there are many subcategories of asshole parenting. One of the biggest is food preparation. It is mostly impossible to get this right with kids. They are offended by everything, from serving the wrong foods to serving it on the wrong plates. I have induced meltdowns for daring to put a vegetable on a child's plate. My daughters protest any food that deviates from the Beige Diet. Herbs are a travesty. Sauces? *How dare you.* And many of us have received the scorn of offering a child their favorite food one meal after it became their unannounced least favorite food.

Hygiene is another opportunity area. There is no sorrow quite like a child being asked to take a bath. Suggest they brush their teeth? You monster. Do they really need to brush their hair or can you just let them live? One would think that by the time you've reached the age of maturation that requires deodorant, a child might be interested in complying with the social norms of not smelling like rotting onions, but one would be wrong. While shame is not a parenting technique I condone, deodorant is one area where I make an exception. I have been known to give my children encouraging and motivational admonishments such as "I am surprised you have friends when you smell like that." I have also picked my children up from school and threatened to make them walk home because the smell was so bad.

We've had lots of fights over clothing in my house. When they were young it revolved around the audacity of me not wanting them to be naked in public. Then it was arguments over my suggestions that they wear weather-appropriate clothing. As they've gotten older, the disappointment has revolved around buying them things that are "lame" and "off-brand" because apparently these children who live with me, who do not earn an income, need to be clothed in attire more expensive than what I put on my own body. I'm also a tyrant because I do not allow my daughters to wear shorts that display their butt cheeks, which is to say, most commercially made shorts for young girls. Thanks, misogyny!

Then there is traveling with children, which provides many opportunities to fail them. I've always said that travel with small children is simply an opportunity for tantrums in new, more expensive places. The proclivity for outrage on a vacation is high, because expectations are often not met, sleep is in short supply, and overstimulation is almost guaranteed. Add to that close quarters and irritating relatives and it's a wonder any of us take children on trips. As a blogger, I've been afforded the opportunity of a lot of inexpensive travel with my kids, which is a huge perk of the job. I can remember taking my children to Machu Picchu, and having to bribe them with M&M's to keep walking. Their overall memory of this wonder of the world is that it was hot. I took my kids on a safari in Tanzania, where my daughter had a meltdown because I asked her to put her iPad away and look out the window at all of the amazing exotic animals instead of watching food videos on So Yummy. And then there was the time we visited Paris, where all four of them whined about the walking and how boring and old everything was.

You might be wondering why I keep trying. I might be wondering the same thing. But travel is a high value for me, and I'm happy to report that on a recent trip to Tokyo with my kids, the ratio of enjoyment to disappointment was about one to one. So . . . progress? Of course this was after my teenagers got over the mortification of going on a family trip in the first place.

For all categories, there are developmental stages to the ways we are assholes to our children, and at this point I've had the good fortune to move through all of them.

GENERALLY PREVENTING THEIR DEMISE: THE TODDLER YEARS

Toddlers have a death wish, and we are the buzzkills in their joyous attempts to maim themselves. Here are some examples of ways I've ruined my toddlers' lives:

- not allowing them to stand on the counter

- requiring them to sit in car seats

- not allowing them to play with dog poop

- not allowing them to eat food they found on the ground

- wiping their butts

- suggesting they wipe their own butts

- wiping running snot from their faces

- removing choking hazards from their mouths

- not allowing them to play with power tools

CHORES AND OTHER FORMS OF OPPRESSION: THE ELEMENTARY YEARS

As kids get older, they are forced to grapple with the indignities of us requiring more responsibility from them. Asking them to pick up a mess they made is an injustice worthy of slammed doors. Suggesting that they read a book or do their homework is likely to illicit eye rolls and heavy sighs. Some other ways we oppress, demoralize, and infuriate them at this age:

- requesting that they do chores

- not understanding the videogame they are talking about

- limiting their screen time

- asking them to take out the trash from the home they live in

- having nothing for them to eat despite both the pantry and fridge being full

- not buying them the "good snacks"

- not buying them a dog

- buying them a dog and then asking them to walk the dog

- being unable to read their minds

- doing the Fortnite dance wrong

- waking them up in the morning

- enforcing bedtime

BREATHING AND OTHER ABUSES: THE TEENAGE YEARS

If you have a teenager, you were probably an asshole to them from the minute their school day ended. Did you pick them up within a visible sight line of their peers? Did you ask about their day? Did you put on music that you like, or worse, did you try to play music *they* like? Did you sing along, or tap a hand on the steering wheel, or slightly nod to the music, or in any way show yourself to be a human being? Ugh. Just stop.

No matter what you've been through or what you've accomplished or what you know, you will *never* understand their complex and their extremely *different* and altogether unique angst. Please stop asking them so many personal questions. Please stop prying into their love lives. Please stop trying to act like you care because you obviously don't even care at all. And don't even pretend like you have been through something similar or have some insight because look at you, you clearly don't know. Also please stop all of the following:

- making eye contact

- breathing

- dressing like you are trying to be young and cool

- dressing like you are old

- attempting to talk to them about crushes or life goals

- not caring about them

- cheering for them at a sporting event

- not being there within two minutes after they called to say they are ready when you live fifteen minutes away

- using memes or attempting to understand memes or simply saying the word "meme"

- making a joke

- trying to give them a hug

- asking them to remove their earbuds at the dinner table

- using words like "lit" and "low-key" and "triggered"

- trying to take their photo

- walking next to them in public

As our kids get older, they begin to stand up to our asshole ways. They develop defenses to the tyranny of our parenting. They protest "I am not a slave" when asked to unload a dishwasher full of plates on which they ate food that you prepared for them. They call out the "hypocrisy" of making them sweep the living room every week when you never do that job. They protest that you are acting like a stalker for inquiring about their well-being or the people they hang out with at the mall. And my personal favorite: "I'm taking a stand against the way you are treating me." *Go ahead, my son. Take that stand. And while you are at it, I'll take back that iPhone in your hand that I pay for.*

AMBIGUITY, FOR SURE

There are times when the adoption process is exhausting and painful and makes you want to scream. But, I am told, so does childbirth.

SCOTT SIMON

So you adopted, and then you got pregnant? That always happens!" This has been said to me by many well-meaning strangers when the conversation turns to children, and it is often said with some level of satisfaction. People love the narrative that after adopting, a person is rewarded with a "real" child.

It always makes me bristle a little bit. I know that most people struggling with infertility will not get pregnant after adopting. Statistically, it happens to a very small few. But the reason this little cliché bothers me is that it implies that pregnancy is a prize or consolation for having adopted. Like adoption is a means to an end. Maybe if you do this selfless act God will reward you with your own child. India was not the "prize" for having adopted Jafta. *Jafta* is the prize for having adopted Jafta.

I suggest that we do away with this little statement altogether. That we let it fly away on the wind with other statements you should never say to adoptive parents. Like "Are those your real kids?" or "How much did he cost?" Or, my favorite, "Do you run a daycare from your home?"

I did adopt twice and get pregnant twice. But, technically, I also got pregnant six other times, and I got pregnant in the middle of two very long adoptions that finalized years after both babies were born. It was all kind of messy and nonlinear, and really stressful.

When I got pregnant with India, it was my fifth pregnancy. I had toddler-aged Jafta running around, and was in the process of adopting him, a process that wasn't going as smoothly as I'd expected. I had lost so many pregnancies that I was more annoyed than hopeful. *I really don't have the bandwidth for another miscarriage right now* was my reaction to the two pink lines this time.

A couple weeks passed, and then a few months, and I was still steeled for loss. I remember Dr. Werlin saying to me at some point in my second trimester, as he was watching a healthy heartbeat flashing back at us on the monitor, "You do realize this one is gonna end with a baby?" I couldn't even process his words. "Kristen, I know you've been through a lot. But I really need you to get your head in the game here. You're well past the point of whatever caused your losses before. You need to start planning to have a baby."

The previous miscarriages, the difficulty adopting Jafta, had left me numb. Why set myself up for another disappointment? But I knew that I needed to heed his words. I had longed to be pregnant, and I was, and detaching from it wasn't fair to me or the baby. I had to find a balance between getting my hopes up and grieving a loss that hadn't happened yet. I had to live in the ambiguity. Man, that was difficult for me.

That pregnancy was an exercise in finding hope again, and in allowing that to prevail over fear. My anxiety was a steady bedfellow throughout the pregnancy. I tried to alleviate some of my anxiety by working with a very attentive midwife and developing a birthplan that I felt good about. This helped me feel like I had some control. Although women who have been through labor know that there is very little about the experience you can control.

I had decided I wanted a water birth. I paid extra to have one set up. I arrived at the hospital and got into the tub, and five minutes in decided I hated it. I felt like an untethered buoy bouncing in the water. My limbs were floating around and at every contraction, I wanted to be still and hold on to something. I couldn't get comfortable. So I got out and spent the rest of my labor in the bed.

As labor intensified, so did the pinching feeling in my cervix. It was a really familiar feeling; it felt like I was having a miscarriage. As it continued, I started to panic. Why was I feeling this pain? Why did it feel exactly the same way? Was this happening again? I finally said something to my midwife about it. "This really feels like my miscarriages. I'm freaking out. It feels the same." She stroked my arm as she gently explained to me, *This feeling is labor. The feeling you had before is labor. This one will be different.*

And it was. Several hours later I experienced the unique and thrilling joy of delivering a baby into the world. It was a staggeringly beautiful experience. I held India and wept with joy, and with relief.

Later, I would waddle to the bathroom and weep from the searing pain in my undercarriage. I would stare at myself in the mirror, in my hospital gown and mesh panties, and mouth the words, *"Never do this again."* I wanted to commit that pain to memory, in case the cuteness of a baby ever tempted me to endure this again.

It did. Sort of.

Getting pregnant with Karis was a surprise. This was my eighth pregnancy. We were open to more kids, but after having India I'd had two more miscarriages. Once again, the pregnancy test barely registered with my emotions. Once again, Dr. Werlin had to talk to me about getting my head together because I was really having a baby. Once I hit the second trimester, I graduated from his fertility office to a regular ob-gyn.

I struggled with anxiety with both of my full-term pregnancies, but it was particularly debilitating with Karis. I spent the first trimester fearing miscarriage, and the last trimester in fear of a diagnosis. A screening test I took flagged that pregnancy with a high likelihood of Down Syndrome.

My new ob-gyn recommended that I have an amniocentesis to confirm, but because it had a small risk of miscarriage, I didn't feel comfortable taking the test. This was only the second pregnancy out of eight that I'd carried past the first trimester. I was not interested in anything that could put it at risk, even if it meant I had to live with terrifying ambiguity for a couple months. For me, the need to know wasn't worth the risk of another loss. He referred me to a high-risk specialist.

When I told the high-risk specialist I would not be doing the amniocentesis, she slammed her clipboard down and stormed out of the room while yelling, "Good luck finding a doctor who will do a twenty-week abortion, because it won't be me." Apparently she thought abortion was a foregone conclusion if my baby had Down Syndrome. For me, it wasn't. When I went back to my ob-gyn, I told him this story and expected sympathy, but instead, he questioned me. "Maybe you should spend some time with parents who have adult children with Down Syndrome," he said. "It might change your mind about the test." It felt violating that two professionals communicated an agenda with regard to whether I should carry a child with Down Syndrome to term. Without hearing my own opinion on the matter, both assumed termination was a foregone conclusion if the test came back positive. I knew that life would be very different if Karis had that diagnosis, but I also knew many friends who were parenting amazing kids with Down Syndrome. I was absolutely terrified of that diagnosis. Still, that choice should have been mine to make, and I was frustrated that medical doctors felt the need to influence that decision. It felt like the opposite of choice.

I ended up firing both doctors and finding a doctor who was supportive of my decision to opt out of an amnio. She also understood my anxiety that delivery day might be the day a diagnosis was confirmed. I did my best to summon my lessons about letting go of outcomes, and in the last months of my pregnancy, I made peace with my fears. That's not to say they went away. I knew that having a child with Down Syndrome would have immense challenges, and I thought about it every day. But I walked into the delivery room prepared either way.

My doctor could not have been more kind. She greeted me and whispered that she was aware of the concerns, and told me that she would do a quick inspection as soon as the baby was born. She encouraged me to stay present and focused on the delivery. I did, and when Karis was born, the doctor made a quick check, laid her on my chest, and whispered in my ear, "I see no signs of Down Syndrome."

I cried in relief, but then also felt shame at my relief. Like I was somehow betraying the validity of the lives of the kids with Down Syndrome that I knew, in the same way the doctors who had questioned me were.

I feel sadness when I think about the detachment I experienced during the pregnancies that resulted in my two daughters compared with the excitement I felt during the first few pregnancies that I lost. My miscarriages robbed me of the simple joys of pregnancy. That's what fear does to us—it robs us of future joy. I regret that, but I don't feel guilt about it. I've had to forgive that version of myself. She was doing the best she could.

The anxiety I felt during my pregnancy didn't go away as soon as I gave birth. Fear, worry, and panic had become habitual for me. The concerns I had about carrying a baby to term just spilled over into fears that Karis was dying, or suffering from a disease or disorder, and that I was not a good mom.

It is normal to be anxious as a mom. It is the biggest life change any of us will ever face, followed by a massive swing in hormones, all fueled by exhaustion and lack of sleep. I think every mom feels a bit panicky as they learn how to navigate life in a new role. For some of us, though, postpartum anxiety becomes crippling. It creeps into every interaction. It makes us fear being around people. It makes us fear being alone. It makes us afraid for our baby. It makes us want to hide. It gives us persistent and intrusive thoughts that we aren't okay, that our baby is not okay, and that we aren't going to make it.

A history of anxiety can make some women predisposed to postpartum anxiety. A history of loss can, as well. I had both, and I was fighting a real battle with irrationally obsessing over Karis's health for the first year of her life. I had struggled with this some after having India, but it was much worse with Karis.

For example, Karis had a particularly dramatic Moro reflex,

which is that little startle reflex babies do when they have an occasional loss of balance or feeling of falling. Karis's startle reflex was pronounced. In my compromised postpartum brain, I decided it was a seizure. And that she was having multiple seizures a day. I then went down a rabbit trail on Google and diagnosed her with a fatal seizure disorder. She eventually outgrew the Moro reflex, but it took a little more time for me to outgrow the postpartum anxiety.

Over her first few years my anxious brain diagnosed Karis with any number of fatal illnesses, from malaria to spinal meningitis. I spent many evenings searching for explanations to minor symptoms and falling down a rabbit hole of terrible outcomes. New moms: Google is not your friend.

If you are struggling and your best efforts are not quieting the brain spin of postpartum depression or anxiety, you know what might be your friend? Therapy. Or medication. Or both. It was for me. I spent far too long convinced that I had to wait to take anxiety meds because I felt pressure to breastfeed for a full year. Breastfeeding is awesome. But so is mental health. In retrospect, I wish I'd given myself permission to prioritize my own health sooner. My kids are now grown, healthy tweens and teens, two who were breastfed and two who were not, and I can't believe I delayed treating my anxiety with medication because of breastfeeding.

Sometimes we have to abandon the ideals we bring into motherhood to make sure that we tend to ourselves. There is truth to the line "put your own airplane mask on first" when it comes to parenting. That might look like letting go of a birthplan, or forgiving yourself for feeling ambivalent, or letting the baby sleep in your bed to get more sleep. Or letting the baby sleep in a crib to get more sleep. *Or whatever you find that works to get more sleep.* It might look like taking a shower while a baby cries, or eating a burrito and cleaning crumbs off an infant's head while you breastfeed, or not breastfeeding at all. And it might look like making that appointment and saying to a doctor . . . I need help.

A healthy, stable mom is what is best for the baby. Full stop.

BUT THEY ARE SUCH
CUTE LITTLE NARCISSISTS . . .

They're awful people.
They're tiny, tiny little Hitlers, all of them.

DONALD GLOVER

If I had to sum up motherhood in one philosophical statement it would be this: They come out of the womb as narcissists,
and you have eighteen years to try to change that. If, by the time
they move out of your house, they are able to consider others
with some level of empathy, attend to the feelings of others, and
see the world outside themselves and the people who inhabit it
as valid and important, you've done your job.

Most people dislike the idea of their own kid being a narcissist, but hear me out. Babies have absolutely no concept of
thinking about how others are feeling. In fact, developmentally,
at first they don't even understand that other people are sepa-

rate from them. Other people function only to meet their needs, be it food, comfort, or changing.

I found parenting newborns to be particularly difficult because they don't give you much positive feedback. My first child joined our family at six months old. On my first day as a mom, he was reacting to me (and sleeping through the night . . . can I get an amen?). He would smile and laugh, he would giggle and coo. Sure, he was also mostly concerned with his own needs. But at least he was giving me *something*.

Then I got pregnant and had a baby the way that involves having your lady parts rearranged and your midsection blown up beyond recognition and your hormones staging a coup against your brain. All of this coming after months of discomfort, heartburn, weight gain, and waddling. I found pregnancy to be incredibly uncomfortable, and at some point I began jokingly referring to my baby as my "parasitic being." Listen, mocking is my love language. And I started early with my children.

On one particularly difficult day, I was sitting on the sofa feeding my newborn, feeling completely trapped by this ten-pound human who never smiled and barely interacted with me except to cry, poop, and eat. I said to my husband, "It's like she's *still* a little parasite!" And you might be reading this and thinking, *How could you say that about your children?* But you know what? *Every newborn ever is a selfish needy blob.* Even you were. Babies' only interest in life is getting their needs met by others. And our job as parents is to make sure they grow out of it.

It's developmentally normal that babies are self-centered and demanding. But that doesn't make it any easier when you are a tired new mom and just want to sit down already and you hear that shrill dolphin newborn cry bidding you to get up and change a diaper.

Most of my worst moments happened when trying to get my babies to sleep. I spent many a night with my hand on the back of a newborn in their crib, willing them to stop crying, only for them to start crying the minute I removed my hand and started to creep toward the door. *Why do they need me here? Why is this baby so codependent? Why won't she just let me sleep? This baby has no respect for my boundaries.* These are the irrational things I found myself thinking in those desperate, sleep-deprived moments.

Babies are completely oblivious to your feelings, and then they turn into toddlers. Toddlers are not just narcissists, they are also psychopaths. They maintain all the self-centeredness of a newborn, buttressed by mind games and limit-testing! Their lives revolve around meeting their own needs *and* trying the bounds of your own emotional regulation.

When my kids were toddlers, we had a cutting-edge TV that had a DVD and a VCR built in. (Yes, I'm dating myself. I'm also old enough that I used the Internet for the first time after graduating from college. Shout-out to microfiche!) Anyway, the slots for the VCR and DVD were right at eye-level for a curious toddler, and it quickly became their favorite toy. They loved to sit and push on the VCR flap. But the real payoff feature was the DVD slot. You push that eject button, and a thing slides out, often a DVD that you can now play with.

The DVD function got broken by toddler shenanigans more times than I can count, and it became a battle of wills with every toddler that lived in my house (which, if you are keeping count means for about six consecutive years). Every day was an opportunity for them to defy me, get past me, and push that precious button.

At some point, every single one of my kids had a showdown with me that involved me looking straight at them, reminding them *the answer is no,* and them proceeding to push the DVD button while making direct eye contact with me as if to say, *I see you, bitch. What are you going to do about it?* And really, what *was* I going to do about it? I mean, the global move away from spanking has been humane and psychologically appropriate, but it has left us kind of impotent in these moments, hasn't it?

The life mission of a toddler is to get a rise out of you and watch you lose control. Intentionally throwing their plate of food and then crying that they no longer have said food is a toddler's idea of family bonding. Dropping a toy from the grocery cart and then screaming until you pick it up and hand it back, over and over and over again, is a thing toddlers would list on their résumé under "hobbies and special interests." Imagine if an adult were engaging in this behavior: throwing something for no reason, requiring another person to pick it up, doing it over and over again, and screaming if the cycle stopped. We would label that person a sociopath. If you vetted the behavior of a toddler against a checklist of a "toxic person," they would check every single box. When people ask me how to survive the toddler years, I literally shrug and say, "I don't know, man. Just survive." This book is 100 percent free of advice for how to manage a toddler because I have none, except to just power through it and know that it is universally awful.

But then they emerge from the infant narcissism and the toddler psychopathology and become kids who are observant, sometimes kind, and often thoughtful. They begin to notice your feelings and sometimes even try to attend to them. They reflect back what you say. They are reciprocal in conversations. They try to comfort you. They initiate hugs and affirmations. They aren't perfect, but you start to see the glimpses of an emotionally attentive person in them.

Age five-ish to about twelve . . . these are the golden years of parenting. A small but beautiful window where you are not regularly wanting to cry or drink because of their behavior. A time when kids are cuddly and cute and delightful, at least some of the time. And then they become teenagers.

I know there are many theories of child development floating around, from Piaget to Freud. But I'd like to postulate my own developmental framework.

STAGES OF PARENTING

Age 0–2: Keep them from putting something in their mouths they can choke on.

Age 3–5: Keep them from falling from heights that could maim or kill them.

Age 6–12: Brief window of reciprocal parent-child enjoyment.

Age 13–18: Keep them from doing drugs, looking at porn, or making you a grandparent.

This Mother's Day, I woke up to four kids giggling excitedly outside my door. They knocked and entered, with a tray full of breakfast for me. They'd made my eggs over medium, just the way I like them. They'd toasted me some gluten-free bread. They'd brewed my favorite tea. There were little finger trays of perfectly arranged fruit, and there was a vase with a rose from my front yard. They had each made me a card and coupon book for future acts of service. And they had done all of this on their own, without help and with absolutely no money. Every aspect had been thoughtfully and carefully planned and executed by my former needy parasitic blobs, and I had one of those hard-earned moments of parenthood when I thought, *Maybe I'm not totally bungling this.*

SMELLS LIKE TEEN SPIRIT

To an adolescent, there is nothing in the world
more embarrassing than a parent.

DAVE BARRY

While infants may meet the diagnostic criteria for narcissism and toddlers may tick off the symptoms of sociopaths, teenagers and their hormones often mimic the symptoms of rapid-cycling bipolar disorder. True story: Therapists are warned against diagnosing borderline personality disorder in teens because the symptoms of JUST BEING A TEENAGER can create a false diagnosis.

Teenagers are not here for your feelings. Any empathy that you may have seen emerge in previous years takes a backseat to two insidious factors that will overwhelm your child's brain: hormones, and an obsessive concern with peer acceptance. Teens *can* display empathy, but it's probably not for you. They can have hours of patience listening to their friend Ava describe her heartbreak at the end of a serious two-week relationship, but they have no interest in hearing about how their eye-rolling and persistent lying make you feel sad and disrespected. Teens are inherently self-centered. Their primary interest in you is that of taxi driver and ATM machine.

Developing empathy promotes many of the other character traits we want our kids to learn, like social skills, honesty, loyalty, and kindness. Good grades are great. Athletic awards are fun. But it's the moments my kids show true empathy that I feel the most proud of them.

My oldest is deep in the teen angst, but every once in a while I see a glimmer of thoughtfulness that gives me hope. The other day we pulled into a parking garage and parked next to a big Ford pickup truck. My teenager noticed that there was a metered ticket to the parking garage lying on the ground next to the truck, and wondered if it might belong to the truck owner. "Man, it would really suck if that driver lost his ticket," he observed. "He'd have to pay thirty bucks even if he was just here for an hour." We walked about halfway to our destination from the parking garage, and he turned back. "I'm just worried he may not see the ticket on the ground. I'm gonna go put it on his windshield to make sure." He was worried about a stranger. And that little glimpse into his concern for another person made me more proud than any accolade he could receive.

I think that sometimes in our parenting hierarchy empathy is relegated to the backseat in the quest to make sure our kids feel good about themselves. Self-esteem is important. But I'm a subscriber to the idea of empathetic self-esteem. Empathetic self-esteem allows us to love ourselves *and* to love others. It also requires insight and reflection. It's not a blind self-esteem that says, "I'm great because I'm great!" It's a reflective self-esteem that takes into account the ability to be wrong, the reality of mistakes, and the quest for self-improvement. Empathetic self-esteem considers not only self but others.

There are a lot of mantras going around these days about how "other people's feelings about you are none of your business." There are mantras about not owning the feelings of others, or about not having to apologize. I get it. As a lifelong codependent I can see where I have spent way too many hours worrying about what others think or if someone is upset with me. I don't think we need to concern ourselves with the opinions or feelings of every person we know. We don't need to morph ourselves into being liked by everyone. However, I do want my kids to be concerned with how they are making the people in their inner circle feel. I don't want them to have an entitled self-esteem that is unable to consider feedback. If their younger sibling feels they are a bully, I want them to be concerned with that. If their reputation among their close friends is for being a backstabbing mean girl, I want them to be concerned with that. We should all be mindful of how the trusted people in our inner circle experience us, because sometimes we need that mirror to see ourselves clearly.

It can be uncomfortable to watch our kids sit with feelings of conviction or guilt about their own behavior. So we try to save them from their sadness with platitudes and praise. It's easy to say, "If Suzie doesn't like you, then forget her! She's a meanie!" It's harder to help our kids examine how they may have played a part in the situation.

The balance between shaming our kids and bringing them to a healthy understanding of their own culpability is a tricky one. I have certainly landed on the latter, especially as it relates to body odor, in which my tendency to use shame as a parenting tool might look like saying, "I feel like your teachers have to be talking behind your back about how bad you smell." Listen, I'm not always doing it right. But I'm convinced that awareness and conviction is required for true empathy.

In my experience, the key lies in addressing behaviors, not character. It's the difference between saying, "You are mean," and, "How do you think your sister feels about you breaking her doll and then hiding it? What must that be like for her?" The latter addresses observable behaviors. It doesn't actually assign blame or point out a character defect, it simply states a behavior and then asks the child to consider the effect. I think a key element of teaching awareness and empathy is avoiding blame and lectures. Instead we should try to reflect on what we observe and ask our kids to do the emotional labor of considering how their behaviors have affected others. I don't want my kids to feel responsible for every feeling someone else has but when it's clear that they have done something that was hurtful or unfair, I want them to sit in that discomfort. And similarly, when they've done something that has clearly been affirming or generous to someone else, I also want them to sit in that experience.

My kids and I are working on acknowledging and attending to the feelings of the people closest to us—and when I see them doing that, I feel like I'm doing something right.

IS YOU IS OR
IS YOU AIN'T MY BABY

Worry does not empty tomorrow of its sorrow,
it empties today of its strength.

CORRIE TEN BOOM

My road to motherhood was rocky. Infertility was followed by miscarriages, and then, we adopted. Except . . . that part isn't entirely true. For about six months after bringing Jafta home I lived in the bliss of believing I would soon be adopting him. Then I got a call from his social worker that would put my role as Jafta's mom into question for the next three years.

Jafta's adoption was supposed to be what the state of California refers to as a "fast-track adoption." We were technically foster parents, but the process would move to adoption quickly because the state had terminated reunification services for his birthparents. Typically, when children enter foster care, the state offers reunification services in an effort to help parents reunite with their children. In rare cases, where there have been repeated abuse or neglect charges with previous children, re-unification services are terminated early or not offered at all. That was the case with Jafta. When Jafta's birthmom was discovered to be pregnant, the court determined that the baby would be taken into care immediately, and placed for adoption.

One afternoon, while one-year-old Jafta was napping, I recognized the social services number from Compton ringing on my phone, so I picked it up. It was our social worker, Dorothy. She wanted us to come into her office to discuss things, because "we might have a *Losing Isaiah* situation on our hands." I asked her what that meant, knowing she was referencing a movie where an adoptive parent had to return a child. "We will need to discuss it in person," she said. We set a time to meet and I panicked. After losing so many babies to miscarriages, could I lose this baby, too? It was a week between that phone call and our meeting. That week I had the same feeling of dread that I experienced the week I waited between my fourth miscarriage and meeting with Dr. Werlin. I imagined every possible outcome, and I would soon find out that my worst fears were a possibility.

We met with Dorothy and she explained that a biological relative had just come forward and offered to take Jafta. I was devastated. Jafta had been in foster care for a year, first with the sweet elderly woman who cared for him as an infant and then with us. This relative knew he had been taken into care. She'd been asked to take him when he was first removed from his birthparents. Why was she just showing up now?

I was angry, but also in a state of cognitive dissonance. I believe that children should not be separated from their birth family unless there is severe risk to the child's safety. I believe in open adoption, and that keeping ties to biological family are important.

But when I found out who it was, I was upset. I recognized her name because it was all over the report I'd been given about his birthmom's case history. This relative had a long record of her own with child protective services. I did not understand why social services would want to give Jafta to a relative with her history when he had two loving parents that he was already bonded to. He didn't even know her.

Fortunately, it isn't up to biased and emotional foster parents to determine outcomes for children in these very complicated scenarios. There are social workers and court advocates and judges who are tasked with objectively putting the rights of children first. This is good. But it didn't feel good to live through. I loved this child as my own, and yet had no control over his fate.

I was a wreck. I had weathered the storm of trying and failing to be a mom for so many years, and I had finally become one. I remember wondering, as we drove home from that meeting with Jafta in his car seat behind me, *If he leaves, am I still a mom? What am I then?*

I didn't know how to process this news. I lived every day in fear of Jafta being taken away. I thought about it while I pushed him on the swings, while I fed him his bottle, while I read him to sleep. *Is this boy my son?*

My brain started grieving every possible terrible outcome, so that if it happened, I would be prepared for it. Obviously, this is utter bullshit because (a) hypothetical preparation does not hasten the grief process when there is actual loss, and (b) all this did was put me into a state of mourning until I knew the outcome. It's catastrophizing and preemptive grief, and it's a terrible way to live. But it proved hard to escape that loop in my head. When I looked at my son, I saw someone I loved. Simultaneously, I saw the possibility of the greatest loss I had ever known.

Someone gave me the advice that I needed to love Jafta with an open hand. And I tried my best to do that. I went through the motions of motherhood and bonding. I tried to love "as if." I tried pretending that this giant question mark over my role in his life was not there, or that it didn't matter. I'd like to think that outwardly, I succeeded. Jafta was lavished with love, cuddles, and attention. Inside, my heart was breaking daily. But every new day I asked myself, "What would a loving mother do today?" and that is what I did.

I had to will myself to behave like a mother who was not enveloped in fear. Slowly, the more I actively loved him, the more my anxiety decreased. Eventually I was able to simply focus on my love for him, and not the fear of losing him, for larger chunks of the day.

During this season, I saw the play *Wicked,* and there was a song called "For Good" that spoke about the idea of temporary love, of the power of a season with another person and how much we can be changed by them.

> *I've heard it said that people come into our lives for a*
> *reason*
> *Bringing something we must learn*

This song became my anthem for my relationship with Jafta. Regardless of how the story ended, I would make a difference in his life, and he would change mine. I sang it to him every single night, through tears, willing myself to love him the best I could regardless of how things might end.

I would later learn that this exercise of choosing love over fear with our children is ongoing. My tendency to worry over my children would threaten to paralyze me in matters big and small for many years to come. It's so easy to obsess over outcomes for our kids that it has almost become a norm of motherhood. We receive so many messages that parenting is about moving forward with some ambitious plan for their lives. Get them in the right club sports so they can play in college. Get them in the right schools so they can go to the right college. Make sure they are successful, measured by whatever external yardstick we've chosen.

While we all want to give our children the best chance in life, it's a fine line between encouraging our kids to thrive and needing to control their outcomes. When I find myself in that spiral of fear over their futures, I remind myself of the lessons learned in this season. Love isn't about planning for the future, it's about presence. We are never promised tomorrow. We are never promised that our children's lives will be easy or free of heartbreak, disease, addiction, or mental illness. Our children will inevitably make choices and experience pain and losses that will take our breath away. And the only answer in those situations is to love well, today.

Jafta started to crawl, and then started to walk. He learned his first words, and I tried to stifle the panic and fear as he began to call me "mama." I tried to continue in the activities of normal motherhood while we waited to hear what was going to happen with his relative. We did playdates. We celebrated birthdays and holidays. Love over fear. This was my daily task.

During this wait, I gave birth to India. Big brother Jafta was absolutely thrilled with his new baby sister. Jafta talked incessantly about the things he and India would do together. Most of these things required her being quite a bit older; they would ride bikes together and play sports together. He was dreaming of a future with his sister, with our family. And I was still waiting to find out if they would be lifelong siblings, or if India and Jafta would lose each other, too.

As a first-time mom, I was excited to make Jafta a baby book. I'm a memory keeper by nature and have carefully curated scrapbooks of every stage of my life. I wanted to give that to my kids. Yet, working on his was so fraught. His baby book seemed like a huge symbol of our family's potential loss. As I worked on it over those years of uncertainty, I would wonder what I would do with the baby book if he was taken from us. Would I send it with him? Would I keep it? If I gave it to his relative, would she even show it to him? If I kept it, would I be able to look at it again?

Making his baby book also brought up other fears. What if he never remembered us? What if all of these memories I had with this child were never known to him? Who would he become apart from our loving family, and what would that separation do to him? It was even painful looking at family portraits back then. The questions about Jafta's future lasted well into his younger sister's first year of life. I used to wonder if someday India would look at these pictures and not recognize or remember the boy sitting next to her. I even had the awful thought, during those years, that perhaps we should be taking separate family portraits without him, just in case. So we would not have a three-year string of family photos that were a painful reminder of a child we lost.

Month after month, there was no news. Three years in, Jafta was still my foster child. He didn't share my last name. I had to get permission to take him on family trips. I wasn't allowed to cut his hair. There were constant reminders that I wasn't his mother, only a temporary guardian. I had to push all of these details aside. Love. Love was the only path forward. Love was the only thing I could do. It was the only thing I could control. And if he went back, I would never regret having loved him well.

Finally, we attended a court date for Jafta in which his case was reviewed. We'd been to so many of these court dates and often left with less information than we came with. A case-worker was present, and reminded the judge that a relative was seeking custody. The judge peered through his glasses at the documents that were turned in. "But this relative has failed to file her paperwork for two years?" He was clearly disgusted. And in one metaphorical bang of the gavel, the judge ruled that the relative was no longer an option, and that Jafta should be adopted by us.

The day we were finally able to adopt Jafta we drove up to the L.A. family court knowing that we were going there to *finalize*. We had made that trip so many times in the last three years, and every time it had been with a feeling of dread and anxiety as other people made decisions about the future of this boy we loved. On our way, I realized it was the first time that I didn't have a stomachache as we approached the court. It was the first time I wasn't petitioning God in prayer as we waited for our name to be called.

It was also a stark contrast inside the courtroom. Instead of feeling alone and intimidated, we had a room full of family and friends there to back us up, and we felt confident and supported as a family. It was emotionally overwhelming. As soon as the judge had us raise our right hands and state our names, I was fighting the ugly cry. And losing.

We were asked to confirm that we wanted to adopt him, and then asked if we vowed to love him and treat him as we would any biological child. As we sat there with India, our little sur-prise in the midst of this journey, I knew full well that we did love Jafta as if he were our own biological child. When she an-nounced he was now officially Jafta Jordan Howerton, the room erupted in applause.

I am grateful that I learned to love Jafta regardless of outcomes, and I would still feel grateful even if he had not stayed with me. For as long as I could remember, I had used anxiety to protect my heart against the possibility of pain. But fear is such an ineffective anesthetic. It hadn't worked with the years of infertility and miscarriages, and it didn't work during Jafta's long adoption journey. What happened in those years of loving a child who might not ever be mine was that I learned—later than some, earlier than others—how to love fiercely in the here and the now. This is all any of us can really do for the people we hold dear. We trudge along in this human experience, looking for connection while simultaneously facing our fears around loss or rejection or emotional distance. Regardless of the circumstances, none of us are guaranteed outcomes with the people we love. So all we can do is love our people well, even in the face of knowing that nothing is ever certain.

Once his adoption was final, I completed Jafta's baby book, and I found myself sobbing as I thought of the tightness in my chest I had felt when I'd started it. I allowed myself to look at all the pictures in a new light. I gazed at the family photos of a happy, *permanent* family. I allowed myself to feel grateful that I will be the keeper of this baby book. I will be the one who adds to this catalog of memories. I will be the one who shows embarrassing baby photos to high school sweethearts. I will be the mother watching these photos in a wedding slideshow. Finishing that baby book was a symbol to me that I would be his mom forever. Status known.

Some years later, I would watch that little boy graduate from elementary school, singing the song "For Good" along with the rest of his sixth-grade class, a detail of his promotion ceremony that he'd kept from me until that moment. This song that I sang to him every day for three years to express my love for him regardless of outcomes, he was singing as he achieved a milestone of childhood. I bawled as I watched my little baby, now taller than me, stand there in a suit and tie. He had changed me for the better.

THE MYTH OF COLORBLINDNESS

Some well-meaning folks think if we stop talking about racism, it'll magically disappear, like the smell of an errant fart. But like a fart, people might try to be polite and ignore it, but everyone knows it's there. Avoidance has never been a great tactic in solving any problem.

LUVVIE AJAYI

On the day that we took Jafta home from the Department of Children and Family Services in Compton, an older black man, who was a seasoned social worker, sat us down for a talk before our son was given to us. "You do realize, now, that little black boys grow into black men?" My response was defensive. *Of course I know that!* I explained that I was very close to my nephews, who were black, and who were now young men. There is nothing wrong with black men, I assured him. And of course there isn't, but that wasn't his gist. I was just too clueless to know what he meant at the time. Because *love is all you need* and all that.

We hadn't set out to adopt a black child. We were open to any race. But black children are proportionately overrepresented in foster care, and at the time we were adopting, we were one of a handful of prospective adoptive parents in our agency who had checked the box "open to a child of any race." At the time, I fancied myself a strong antiracism advocate. In truth, I was pretty ignorant. We went through all of the requisite trainings and classes meant for adoptive parents and got a couple hours on transracial adoption. We did exercises like putting different colored beads in a jar, with only one black bead in a sea of white, to try to understand what our child might feel like. But did staring at colored beads really allow me to feel the inherent bias and feelings of alienation that come with being a minority? It was a nice visual, but a far cry from the lived experience.

When we first adopted Jafta, I was keenly aware and self-conscious of being a white woman with a black child. It's not that I was embarrassed. In fact, embarrassment might have even been preferable to my actual feelings, which were closer to pride. Jafta was my personal badge of courage, my external and conspicuous proof that I was a kind and caring person and *definitely not racist*. Adopting a black child advertised my compassion and bravery and love for all of God's children. He was my proof that I was a Good Person, a person committed to loving everyone equally. I don't think I would have admitted this at the time, even to myself. But those narratives were there.

This is the naivety that many white people hold—that if we can all just get along, coexist, and love one another, we can solve racism. I thought that transracial adoption was a step toward healing racism because we could be an example to the world that love is colorblind.

I meant well, but the road to hell is paved with white people who mean well.

With Jafta, I became aware of the optics of my *own* race for the first time in my life. This is a hallmark of whiteness in America. Being the majority race, most white people inadvertently consider our own experience as the "default." As a result, we rarely have to confront our own race, and this can cause us to struggle with affirming or even noticing the experiences of people of color.

When we adopted a second time, I had the sense that giving Jafta a racially matched sibling was important. He was a minority in our own home and a minority in our community. By three, he'd begun to make observations about how he "did not match" the rest of the family. I sensed some anxiety there, and wanted to give him a sibling who mirrored his own racial identity. His brother, Kembe, joined our family a few years later. Kembe was adopted from Haiti, and while he still identifies with his Haitian roots, Kembe also identifies as black and American. These shared identities among the brothers have helped them feel less alienated.

When they were four and five years old, I signed my three older kids up for a preschool-aged basketball class. It was our first experience with organized sports (and India's last—*I tried*). The class was held at an upscale community center in a nearby town. As soon as I pulled up, I got a knot in my stomach. I just had this feeling—an intuition—that this might not be the most welcoming place for my two black kids. I literally had this thought as I walked through the door, and I quickly tried to put my cynicism and paranoia in check.

The other kids started arriving, and everyone played for a bit. India was suddenly feeling shy and clingy, so I was standing in the middle of the court, holding baby Karis while trying to loosen India's grip on my pant leg and coax her to stand with her brothers and the other players. Most parents were in the bleachers. There were two young coaches, and they called for all of the kids to circle up and hold hands.

That was when things started to move in slow motion.

I saw Jafta grab the hand of a boy nearby. We'll call him Jimmy. Jimmy looked at Jafta, laughed nervously, and said, "That's a black kid!" Okay, no harm. *He is a black kid.* But then Kembe tried to hold Jimmy's other hand, and Jimmy refused, saying, "Another black kid? I don't want to hold hands with another black kid!"

I was horrified. I looked at the coaches, but couldn't tell if they had heard. Another kid moved into the line and grabbed Jimmy's hand. He reluctantly remained holding hands with Jafta. I was worried about what my boys were thinking or feeling, but they didn't seem to register the incident. Jafta was busy watching the coach. Kembe looked clueless. Since he was still learning English, I don't think he understood. Crisis averted. Sort of?

But then another boy entered the group. We'll call him Timmy. Kembe was standing there looking to hold hands with someone, at the only opening in the circle. Timmy was nearby, and the coaches encouraged him to grab Kembe's hand. Timmy said, verbatim, "No! I don't like the brown. I don't want to hold hands with the brown kid."

I was stunned. I said, to no one in particular, "We can all hold hands with each other, no matter what color." One of the coaches coaxed him to hold hands with Kembe. He was still protesting, but held his hand and finally quieted down when the coaches started talking.

At this point, I was having one of those moments when you can feel the back of your neck getting hot, and your heart rate increasing. I was angry this was happening. And also, really hurt for my kids. The slights seemed to have gone unnoticed by both boys, but I wasn't sure, and I didn't want it to happen again. I took a deep breath and identified the parents of Jimmy. Once the kids were distracted and playing, I approached Jimmy's dad and quietly told him what happened. Jimmy's dad got immediately defensive. He told me I was wrong, that it hadn't happened, even though he wasn't standing close enough to hear the incident. Jimmy's mom approached and when she heard what I was saying, she got even more hostile. She basically took a "how dare you suggest my son is a racist" approach. I tried to calmly tell her that I didn't call him a racist, nor did I think it was an indictment on her parenting or a reflection of their views.

Jimmy's mother's next response, in my opinion, illustrates the root of the problem. She told me that her son has always been instructed to never talk about another person's skin color—so she was having a hard time believing that he said out loud that my son was black. At this point I might have lost my patience a bit, and through gritted teeth I reminded her that he *is* black, and that pointing out that he is black is perfectly fine with me and *not an insult*. What was insulting is the fact that he didn't want to hold the hand of another child because he is black. Probably because he has been taught at home that saying someone is black or brown is something taboo. Therefore, the message sent is that people of color are inherently problematic and scary. Too scary to even talk about or name.

It's not just parents who can be in a lot of denial that this stuff happens. I've sat in a parent-teacher conference where a preschool teacher patted my hand and assured me that "Kids don't notice color," or, "These are all really sweet kids from good families. Racism has to be taught."

Okay, can we all just circle up for a moment and finally put this narrative to rest? No, racism in the preschool set does *not* have to be taught. A kid does not have to have a parent who flies a Confederate flag and openly uses the N word to do something cruel or stupid to a child of color. Any more than a kid who makes fun of someone for wearing glasses means that his parents must hate people who wear glasses. *Sometimes good kids from non-racist homes can have moments of being terrible.* It does not serve anyone to believe the fantasy that a child cannot spontaneously exclude or insult another child for their skin color unless their parents taught them to do so. Sometimes it happens as an experiment in exclusion and difference. And sometimes it's learned—not from parents but from society. Racism is embedded in the systems of our everyday lives. Kids pick up on the subtle and unfair hierarchies that stem from those conditions. It happens. Way more than we want to believe. And by "we" I mean white people. Because people of color know this shit goes down, and they are probably quite sick of our denial systems about it.

Even some of my white friends have been uncomfortable looking at, hearing about, or talking about these disparities. I have had many other mothers relate stories to me about how their kids don't notice race, as if this is a confirmation that their children don't hold any prejudice. Countless times, people have recounted adorable anecdotes to me about how their kids didn't even realize Jafta was adopted. Because they just didn't notice his race! Spoiler alert: *They can see his skin is brown.* They just don't understand genetics yet.

I've always been fascinated by how white people try to skirt talking about race. I remember chuckling to myself when people would say, "Is that your son over there, with the blue shirt and jeans?" or, "Is your son the one with dreadlocks?" If my sons were the only two black kids on the playground, why does it seem so weird just to cut to the chase and say, "Mine are the two black boys."

Yet the few times I was that direct, people cringed. Why? Why should I need to dance around a descriptive term that we all understand? If your kid "doesn't even notice my son is black" then why can't I describe him that way? Why does it seem crude to describe him in terms of an obvious feature, when everyone else feels fine to describe their children by other obvious features (the redhead, the blonde, the one with brown eyes).

I understand the collective hesitation that white people hold about speaking of race. Many of us had well-meaning parents or teachers who grew up with overt racism and wanted to create a better environment. *Race doesn't matter,* we were told. *Everyone's equal.* Don't notice someone's race, and for heaven's sake, don't talk about it if you do. This is the credo that I think a lot of white people were raised on. Though it's certainly an improvement over the direct racism of some of our grandparents' set, in my opinion it has created a generation of people wearing blinders to the real and ongoing issues of prejudice that people of color deal with. It has also created a society in which mentioning someone's race is deemed offensive, where I'm met with blank stares when I talk about my kids' feelings about being the only black kid in his class at coffee with a bunch of other white moms.

The idea that race doesn't matter is a lovely dream, but the truth is that race *does* matter.

I've had to learn to be more comfortable talking directly about race. It's the only way my family can operate. Here's a benign example. I was standing in a long checkout line at Trader Joe's, and the kids were anxious to go up to the manager's station and get their prized lollipop for having spotted the stuffed dolphin hidden in the store. It was a new store, so the kids weren't as familiar with the layout, but I sent them up by themselves because it was in my line of vision and it makes them feel important to do things on their own. I watched my kids approach the long counter at the front of the store. It had three different windows, all labeled, but my kids were too young to read the sign that designated the lollipop-redeeming spot.

Three people were working behind the counter: a white man, a white woman, and a black man. The black man stood behind the MANAGER'S STATION sign (aka the lollipop counter). After spending way too long trying to figure it out, my kids looked back at me. They wanted help. "Which person do we ask?" they pantomimed. I pointed, but they couldn't tell where I was pointing.

They were about twenty feet away from me in a crowded store, so I had to yell to be heard.

"It's the man!" I yelled.

"Which one?"

"The one in the Hawaiian shirt!" It was Trader Joe's. They were both wearing Hawaiian shirts.

"Which man?" they asked back. *Seriously, Mom. Cut to the chase.*

I knew what I had to do, but I didn't want to do it. I looked around. At least fifteen people were within earshot. They could hear everything I was saying.

"The guy on the right!"

They were young enough to struggle with concepts like *left* and *right*. They still didn't get it. Why couldn't I just say it? It's a descriptor.

I looked around again. I steeled myself.

I said it. Actually, I yelled it.

"THE BLACK GUY!"

My kids nodded. They appreciated my specificity and thought nothing of it. But simultaneously I swear I heard a record scratch as every white person in the checkout line turned to look at me in horror. Me, the woman who dared speak it out loud. Me, who identified someone by his race. I saw some people shake their heads. Others rolled their eyes at my apparent rudeness. The bagger looked embarrassed for me. I regretted having said it.

Culture and race are a part of identity, and when we pretend that we don't see someone's race, or that it doesn't matter to us, in a way we are denying a part of their experience. That doesn't mean we need to overdo it and comment on someone else's race or ethnicity in every encounter. That can be an obnoxious over-correction, and I've been witness to it.

For example, for a season I was in a job setting where I worked closely with five other people. All members of the group where white, except for Jill. Another group member had a habit of continually pointing out how "white" she was when Jill was around, or contrasting her lack of proficiency in black slang with Jill's. She didn't do this to anyone else in the group. The result was that she often infused race into everyday interactions with Jill in a way that was unnecessary and othering. I believe she was trying to make a connection, but this illustrates the difference between intent and effect. The effect was an uncomfortable belaboring of Jill's race despite good intent. There is a balance between acknowledging, overemphasizing, and ignoring. White people need to learn that balance, and also model it with our children.

Talking about race with our kids is kind of like the sex talk. If we never talk to our kids about sex, they are going to figure it out on their own. Which will probably lead to some not-so-great influences filling in their gaps of knowledge. In our home,

I've made it a point to talk about physical differences, including race and gender, and the importance of rejecting biases and stereotypes based on these differences. I've also tried to infuse my kids with empathy for kids who are learning English, and have introduced them to other cultures, including foods, experiences, art, and religions that are different from our own. Here are a few other suggestions for white parents interested in developing an environment in which diversity is valued:

1. Take an inventory of your home's diversity. Make it a point to buy dolls and action figures of every race. Have a wide variety of books in your home, both featuring characters of other races and countries, and also written by people of color. Be intentional about watching shows with lead characters of diverse backgrounds.

2. Lead by example. Widen your circle of friends and acquaintances to include people from different backgrounds, cultures, and experiences.

3. Look for opportunities to immerse your family in other cultures. Try to find situations where your family is the minority. This is a great stretching and empathy-building opportunity. Try attending a minority church event or a cultural festival. Observe your child's reactions and open a dialogue about how that feels.

4. Watch how your kids play with children who are different, whether it be skin color, gender, disability, or physical differences. Talk about it. Let your child know that you are a safe person to process their feelings and reactions with, while at the same time guiding them to accept children with differences.

5. Take inventory of your own racial biases. Be careful with the language you use around your children. Avoid making stereotypical statements or racial jokes in front of your children. (And really. Just stop doing it altogether. You know better.)

6. Educate yourself on racism and privilege, and keep learning. Read the works of authors like Austin Channing, Ta-Nehisi Coates, Ijeoma Oluo, Moustafa Bayoumi, and Eduardo Bonilla-Silva.

7. Talk about civil rights and heroes of the movement, and when they are mature enough to understand, discuss the specifics of Jim Crow, slavery, the assassination of MLK, and other atrocities based on ethnicity, race, or religion (the Holocaust, the Bosnian War, the Partition of India, the conflict in Syria, to name a few).

8. Continue to discuss current global examples of ethnically motived violence and oppression, issues of social justice, current circumstances of slavery, and all forms of xenophobia.

Children are social beings, and one of the first social lessons they learn is to sort and group. Boys hang out with boys. Girls hang out with girls. If your children show these preferences, chances are they have racial preferences, too. This doesn't necessarily make them little racists. It doesn't mean they have a future in the KKK. It just means that they need some gentle guidance from you to be a little less self-centered. And really, isn't that what parenting is all about? Training our kids to move from a self-centered infant into a more respectful and empathic person. That's the stuff of raising kids.

CHECKING EMAIL IS THE NEW CHURNING BUTTER

You can learn many things from children. How much patience you have, for instance.

FRANKLIN P. JONES

Be present. It's one of those things I hear all the time. We are supposed to be relishing every moment. I used to have older women give me an "encouraging word" at the grocery store when, apparently, I looked a little too haggard or showed my frustration at my child's tantrum in the produce section. "The days are long but the years are short," they would say. Or, "Cherish this time while you can." I remember wondering, during one particular multi-child meltdown in Target, what exactly about that moment I was supposed to be cherishing. The public embarrassment? The stares from others? The juggling act as I tried to keep four children from running away from the cart or lying down and screaming as I tried to grab groceries as quickly as I could? Because I didn't want to be present in that moment. I wanted to be beamed to another dimension.

I love the *theory* of being present with my kids. I've talked about my own journey to move out of fear and into presence. I believe in quality time and quantity time, and I believe that children deserve consistent attention and love. But listen. I cannot be present at every moment. Kids need the freedom to explore and, sometimes, they need the *catalyst of boredom* to explore. Moms (and dads) need to free themselves from the crushing expectation to observe, plan, and cheerlead every moment of their children's lives.

I worry that in the pursuit of better parenting, we've swung the pendulum a bit too far and set up some unrealistic expectations. When my kids were younger I attended a weekly moms' group at my church. It was called Nurture. It was basically a MOPS (Mothers of Preschoolers) group, but at hipster megachurches we are contractually required to change the names of everything to something that sounds edgy. Youth group can't be called youth group, it needs to be called something like ELEVATE or FUEL or ATOMIC or MOMENTUM. (I just got the best idea for a drinking game: *Youth group or energy drink?* You're welcome.) Anyway, it was basically a weekly group of moms that involved breakfast, a speaker, group sharing time, and a craft. I went for the breakfast and the free childcare, and tolerated the speaker and the "accountability time."

The accountability time and the speakers weren't inherently bad. It all just felt a little privileged and simplistic. We had speakers talk to us about the importance of waking up before our children to read the Bible, the importance of putting kids on a schedule, the importance of looking nice for our husbands and having energy for sex (yes, really), and the importance, of course, of being present with our kids.

One of our frequent speakers was a woman who had adult children, one of whom was a famous-y athlete and very public about his faith. As such, many women in the church looked to her as a mentor figure, and she relished this status. Now, I don't have any idea if she was an amazing mom or not. She probably was. But I do feel like sometimes moms who have celebrity kids are bestowed a sort of expert status, and that was certainly the case here. She spoke at Nurture a lot, and one of her resounding admonishments to us was to make sure we were off our cellphones or computers while our children were awake. To her, this was an impenetrable truth and a question of fitness as a mother. She'd actually been known to pull women aside and check in with them on this matter. "Are you staying off your cellphone when those kids are awake?" she would ask with a serious look. (And let's not speak of the privilege inherent in these questions because it assumes women have the luxury of not working.) We young mothers felt dutifully shamed into changing our habits, because what kind of a monster looks at Instagram unless their child is taking a nap.

A few years ago there was a sanctimonious letter making the rounds on the Internet, an open letter to a mother who was looking at her cellphone at the park. The gist was that this mother was missing out on her daughter's childhood by looking at her phone instead of watching her daughter the whole time she was at the park. "What if she did a cartwheel and she missed it?" the concerned author questioned.

I remember reading this and initially feeling shame. But then I became angry. Because, no. This mom-guilt aggression cannot stand.

Look, I appreciate the impulse to encourage parents to be present. That's important. We live in a distracted, technological age and we would all benefit from a good, hard look at how the screens in our lives pull us away from relationships. I'm all for introspection and self-analysis and balance and boundaries. I think our kids deserve our time and attention.

But I can't help thinking that the idea that children require our 100 percent undivided attention 100 percent of the time has gone a little too far. In fact, I would argue that it's a decidedly twenty-first-century, first-world problem to put so much effort into not working on other tasks when our children are around. I think it's bred from the faulty sense that children are so fragile that *not* being watched lovingly 24/7 will lead to lifelong trauma. But I also think sometimes it's not about the children's needs at all, and more about performative mothering, a need to show that you are *always momming so hard.* And it's leading to a lot of entitled kids who don't know how to handle not being the center of attention.

Mothers have had to multitask since the dawn of time. In fact, I can't think of another era or culture where mothers have had the luxury (or pressure) to do nothing but sit and relish what their child is doing at any given moment. Okay, *maybe* some aristocratic mother at some point in history had that privilege. But even then, she probably paid staff to watch the kids while she hosted tea. Watching a child do cartwheels (metaphorical or real) is not a core element of a mother's job. For centuries, "normal" women have had to farm, work, cook, clean, and do laundry. And in the midst of that, of course, loving mothers found time to make meaningful connections with their children. Modern conveniences like dishwashers, washing machines, Instant Pots, and pre-washed, pre-chopped veggies mean that we don't have to spend as much time as Ma from *Little House on the Prairie* on household tasks. But modern conveniences have also shifted the way we spend our time. Checking email is the new churning butter. I don't need to sew a dress today, but I may need to pay bills online. Mothers still have shit that needs to get done.

I decided that I refused to be shamed because some of my weekly duties required me to sit with a laptop or cellphone. From a young age, my kids understood that the world does not always revolve around them. Sometimes other things will require my attention. I'm going to take in moments and make moments with my kids. When my kids were small and I worked from home, we played and snuggled and had fun together. But also, sometimes, I was on my laptop or computer. If you love volunteering in the classroom, more power to you! If you love making elaborate bento-box lunches for your kids every day, you do you. But we need to lower the shame about moms diverting their attention away from their kids for other pursuits, even if that pursuit is staring at a wall and being alone with our thoughts, or watching reality television at night, or getting together with girlfriends to drink wine.

Let's be honest: Not every minute of every day is a Moment. Ain't nobody got time for that many moments. As Ecclesiastes says, there is a time to be precious about your kid's childhood, and a time when you just have to get shit done. (I've loosely paraphrased that verse.) If we make sure to put in the time and attention when it matters, our kids are gonna be all right. It's okay to miss a few cartwheels.

DAD PRIVILEGE

While we, as a society, have had many public discussions
about the gender distribution of housework and childcare, the
mental load is like a phantom—felt by many, but, without the
language to describe it, very difficult to discuss.

LEAH RUPPANNER

One Christmas morning while I was still married, the kids
were excitedly opening their Christmas gifts, and their dad was
expressing surprise at each gift right along with them. "Dude, a
Nerf gun? You are so stoked!" "A *High School Musical* doll? So
lucky!" It occurred to me that he wasn't just playing along or
pretending to be clueless. He genuinely had never seen any of
the gifts under the tree or any of the items in their stockings.
Every single gift was exclusively procured, wrapped, and placed
there by me. He merely showed up on Christmas morning.

That is what I call "dad privilege."

Dad privilege is when you have a repairman in your home all
day, watching you interact with your kids, make lunches, do

laundry, empty lunch boxes, cook dinner, etc. And then your husband comes home in the evening, you leave to run an errand, and the repairman observes your husband interact with the kids for an hour. Then the next morning the repairman enthusiastically goes on and on about how your husband is a hero of a dad because he took care of four kids by himself. *I mean, really! It was amazing how he did that! Wrangling four kids* for an hour *until they went to bed.* Yes. Clearly their father is a hero for caring for his own children briefly while I go to Target.

Or there are the disparate experiences my husband and I had when we took the kids out to eat as a solo parent when they were little. The few times I attempted this, I was stressed the whole time trying to keep the kids quiet to avoid the inevitable side-eye of those around me. But when my husband showed up to our local gourmet taco joint with all four kids in tow they rolled out the red carpet for the Dad Who Takes His Kids Out (alternate title: Dad Who Babysits His Own Children). I'm seen as the mother who couldn't be bothered to cook. He's the super dad who takes the kids out for fun. The waitresses shower him with attention. *They're making a mess? Pssshhht. We'll get that for you!*

Dad privilege is when I go out of town for business and everyone asks who will be "watching the kids." Dad privilege is the fact that, in 2020, there is a role at my kids' school called "room mom" instead of "room parent." Dad privilege is invisible, but it's real. It's a subtle but powerful aspect of an inequity of expectations and mental load when it comes to parenting.

When my own kids were small, there was one day a week that my husband stayed home with them so I could work outside the home. We were both on board with this arrangement, but on those days I often came home feeling guilty. When I walked through the door and saw a tableau of a man cooking dinner with a crying toddler on his hip, I got a gut check that said, *Oh dear. I should be doing that.* And my next thought would be to wonder if he was feeling emasculated. It wasn't rational, but it was there. Because it wasn't a scene I ever observed in my family growing up. And to be honest, it's not a scene I've seen much in movies or in real life, either. In a movie, it's the scene from *Mr. Mom* where Dad doing the housework is the zany gag. Or it's the scene in a drama where a man has to grapple with his wife dying suddenly. It's certainly not an everyday, normal, nothing-to-see-here tableau of family life.

On those days, I worried that my husband would be resentful of doing "women's work." I usually had to talk myself down from that feeling, reminding myself that it was only one day a week, and that my marriage did not adhere to strict gender rules, and that if we were truly egalitarian like we said, this should not be a problem. I believed that, cognitively. So did he. But I often found myself needing to override my initial adverse reaction and consciously step outside of those traditional roles. And so did he.

On those days, he was often vaguely grumpy and resentful. He couldn't come out and say why, because the truth contradicted his stated value of equality. But spending an entire day doing the diapers and the cleaning and the cooking felt off for him, and put him into a foul mood that he didn't give himself permission to speak.

Women of my generation are living in an awkward transition phase when it comes to gender roles and family life. Many of us hold to an ideology that women and men can choose to share both breadwinning and child-rearing responsibilities, and that women no longer need to be passive participants when it comes to big family decisions. We can be equals, in things both domestic and professional. We can split things down the middle. In theory. And many of us entered marriage with this expectation.

At the same time, some of us haven't quite shaken traditional gender norms, either, because it's what we had modeled for us. My mom had a job as a teacher, but on top of that she still attended to all of the traditional domestic duties. I didn't see my dad meal-planning or cooking dinner or cleaning the house or buying our clothes. My dad was not signing us up for activities or keeping the calendar or planning our celebrations. That was Mom's job, on top of her full-time actual job. When we were young, a couple times a week, my dad would comb our hair out after a bath, but that was really the extent of it. The irony is, both my parents viewed him doing this as a major win for equity, because "your grandfathers certainly wouldn't have done this!" Dads in our parents' generation did a couple tasks previously thought of as women's work, and they were afforded a cookie for it. Our mothers still did 89 percent of the work. It was progress, sure. But it wasn't equal.

My generation has wised up to the idea that if both partners work, then both should help with the domestic duties. But living out that value has proved to be tricky.

While my husband and I talked the talk of egalitarian marriage, we came to marriage with subconscious assumptions about how that would play out in the day-to-day. We considered ourselves a co-parenting family. However, it was also hard to get my husband to pitch in on certain things because they were, quite simply, not on his radar. It was not on his radar that "equal" meant he would also need to assist in buying school supplies or washing the sports uniforms between games or volunteering for class parties or buying gifts for teachers or planning birthday parties or making doctors' appointments or cleaning out closets when clothes no longer fit or the hundreds of things that mothers seem to intuitively know need to be done. A lot of us grew up with working dads who really had no clue how much our mothers hustled, how many things they quietly handled that went without notice or praise. And then we get into marriage and feel resentful because our husbands are so completely clueless to all of the details required to keep a family afloat. For me (and I think many of my peers) this puts us in the position of making a choice between (a) reminding/requesting our husbands to pitch in, which feels like nagging, or (b) just doing it ourselves because it's easier.

I would try to talk to my husband about what felt like the inequity of our workload at home, and it always ended up in a fight. He was certain that he was pitching in just as much. I was certain he was not, but the minutiae I attended to in a given week was difficult to quantify, and the tasks were often completed without him even knowing about them. I didn't need fanfare or a cookie because I spent a couple hours filling out forms and washing sheets and buying science project materials. I didn't keep a log of that time, and I didn't talk about it.

The concept of the mental load is one that has only recently gained attention (or even a name) in feminist circles where the inequity of modern family life is causing an often unacknowledged stress. It's an invisible burden that women are bearing. Keeping track of everything at home while also holding down a job requires a level of hypervigilance and multitasking that results in anxiety and overwhelm. And while it may not seem like a big deal, living in a state of continuous partial attention can make us scattered and stressed. It can also raise the tension in the home, as women know something is out of balance but they don't know how to name it or what to do about it. Because in addition to being socialized to *do all of the things,* we've also been socialized that nagging is *very bad*. And the line between nagging and demanding equity in our homes is a tricky one.

My own marriage was plagued by this dynamic. In the rare moments I would get angry and detail how overwhelmed I was, my husband would tell me, "Well, just make me a list, then." Which is a nice thing to offer in theory, but me making him a list still put me in the role of telling him what to do, which I wanted to avoid. What I wanted, rather, was for *him* to make the mental list. He could read the school emails as well as I could. He could add the football games to our shared calendar as well as I could. He could see the piling-up laundry, the burned-out lightbulb, the kids' backpack with a broken zipper. Just once I wanted one of these things to be solved without having to ask first.

There is another sticky aspect to all of this. Men often have more laid-back standards. They seem to be much more capable of letting themselves off the hook, a fact I both resent and envy. Because when you are an egalitarian couple but the kids are dirty or you don't volunteer for the class party or you fail to pitch in for the gala auction basket, it's usually the mom who is judged, not the dad. And often, they are judged by *other women*.

Women, we have our place in reinforcing these gender stereotypes when we hold each other to standards that we don't hold for fathers. Men are not solely responsible for this phenomenon, and women can be just as entrenched and unwilling to abandon these gender roles as men. I don't think all men are entitled assholes. I think most of them genuinely want to help. We are all just living in a messy transition generation that we don't talk about enough, and that we sometimes don't even notice because it's all we know.

This was not the promise of feminism. So how do we equal the scales? Every personal marriage has its own solution, but it starts with open dialogue. For some, it's learning to ask for help from a willing partner who is just oblivious. For others, it's figuring out what each person is good at and delegating roles within each person's strengths. For many of us, it's learning that it's not nagging if we ask for help, and even if our partner thinks that it is, that's okay! You can only change your own narrative. We have to do the inner work to unlearn the old scripts about what men and women are supposed to do, whether our partner joins us in that work or not. That might mean holding men to a higher standard, but it also might mean lowering the ones we hold ourselves to.

OPTING OUT

By saying no to activity, you are actually inviting other aspects of life to the forefront permitting the possibility that the quieter, less vivid, less exciting activity may have a deeper nutritional value.

RUSSELL BRAND

I'm no longer interested in trying to be the World's Best Mom. I'm aiming for World's Okayest Mom.

I'm also no longer interested in trying to raise perfect kids. Because (a) it's not possible, and (b) in my own experience parents trying to raise perfect kids end up raising kids with an anxiety disorder. *Ask me how I know.* I'm content with being a "good enough mom" and raising good enough kids.

There are a number of things that I've decided to opt out of, because I believe that is the only way to sanely do this parenting thing. If we say yes to every supermom standard of conduct, we end up too busy to do any of it well, and certainly too busy to actually enjoy it.

So here are some of the things I've opted out of. This list might be different for you—but make your list or you will drown on the path to the perfectly cut crustless sandwich. In this village of motherhood, we don't *have* to judge each other for making different choices. I can be obsessed with making sure my kids know how to cut an onion properly and you can decide that takeout every night is just fine. We're both good enough moms. And we've got to give each other space to parent differently.

Making Breakfast

My friend Jen is a morning mom. She wakes up cheerful and makes a cooked breakfast for her kids most mornings, and they actually sit down together and eat it. I am the opposite of that. I hate mornings and if I could not speak to another human being until ten A.M., I would be better for it. Breakfast in my house is everyone eating cereal or a granola bar, usually in the car on the way to school. I don't think we have *ever* had a sit-down breakfast unless it was a holiday or something. Another person's child recently inquired about her breakfast options after a sleepover at my house and I told her there was oatmeal, cereal, or eggs. She told me she wanted eggs, and then I told her they were in the fridge, and then we both kind of stared at each other, waiting for the other to make them. And I realized, *Oh. Other mothers make eggs for their children and she's expecting that of me.* I'm not that mom.

Volunteering in the Classroom

There is really nothing I hate more in life than large groups of other people's children. I'm sorry. I love the children of the world . . . from a distance. I find groups of them exhausting. When my kids started school, I felt a lot of pressure to be in the classroom weekly. They attended a magnet school with a *really* high level of parental involvement. There were years when I was the only parent not taking a weekly hour in the classroom, and it was hard to have my kids tell me they wanted me there. But I found that when I volunteered, I came home completely exhausted and worthless for the rest of the day. I also needed to use the time they were at school to do my job, and with four kids at the same school, I just didn't know how to juggle it. Go to all four classrooms every week? Go to each one once every four weeks? And so, with no small amount of guilt, I opted out. And you know what? I have no regrets. I was able to find ways to plug into the school that felt like a good fit for me. I do lots of things behind the scenes. I'm a master at Google docs and sign-up sheets. I run the PTA website. I help organize the school play and the talent show. But I take roles that I can do alone at home. Key word: alone.

But even if I didn't take on those organization roles, I think it's perfectly fine to opt out of volunteering. It's great for moms who have the time, margin, and the personality to enjoy being around a lot of children. I'm so grateful for the moms that do, and I know it is a huge blessing to teachers. But kids will be okay if you, personally, are not in the classroom. If volunteering is your jam, I salute you and thank you. If it's not, I hereby give you permission to abstain.

Clothes Being Folded

This is a bit of a paradoxical opt-out. See, I want my kids to do their own laundry. But in choosing that, it also means their drawers are a hot mess. There's just no way they are gonna fold their clothes anywhere close to acceptable, and I've got to let that go. I make my kids hang most of their clothing because I find that is less difficult to mess up than shoving things in a drawer. T-shirts? Hang them up. Pants? Fold them over a hanger. And then I just will myself not to actually look in the drawers. If I can't see it, it isn't there.

Going to the Store

Some of the most traumatic moments of parenting my kids happened in the aisles of the grocery store or our local Target. So once online shopping and delivery became a thing, I was all over it. I know that it's not great for small businesses or my carbon footprint but you know what it's great for? My sanity. Amazon Prime, Instacart, Postmates, Stitch Fix, if there is a way I can have things mailed to me instead of leaving my house, I'm all about it. "Sorry you are out of toothpaste, kids. You'll have to wait two days for Prime shipping!" Oh well.

Washing Their Sheets As Often As They Should Be Washed

I mean, listen. I'm not proud of everything on this list.

Filling Out . . . Anything

By the time my kids can read, I'm making them fill out all of the forms. I would hereby like to register my complaint at the number of permission slips that come home requiring me to fill out our address, the name of our doctor, our insurance policy number, and our five last residences and three next of kin. Can they really not keep this stuff on file? Do I really need to fill it out for *each new field trip*?

I'm not signing things daily. I'm just not. Piano practice log due on Monday? Bring me that thing Sunday night filled out, and I'll sign my name. I *do* make my kids read every day. But I'm not logging minutes, pages, or signatures on the daily. I absolutely refuse to sign a reading log and make my kids pay attention to what page they started on and what page they ended on because a school wants that on paper. I want my kids to actually *like* reading, which means getting lost in a book, not counting the pages. I am also proud to announce that in 2016, I signed the weekly homework folder for my oldest daughter a grand total of THREE TIMES for the year. I pulled the papers out, sorted them, read them, and threw it away. But signing was just a step too far.

Bringing the "Good Stuff" to the Class Party

I don't want to bake for the class party. I don't even want to go to the store. What I'm *gonna* do? Respond in a flash to that sign-up email and pick plastic utensils or napkins or paper plates or a case of water, which I keep a stash of just for these purposes. Someone else can knock themselves out with the homemade cookies. I will be the napkin underdog all day, every day.

Worrying about Their Wardrobe

I gave up on this a long time ago. When they were toddlers, on any given day I might have one kid in a princess dress, one wearing a cape and just underwear, and another in a Darth Vader mask and board shorts. I have one child who, to this day, refuses to wear anything but shorts regardless of the weather. Another child reeeeallly loves pairing plaid with stripes. Yearbook photo? I see that you wore that old hoodie with holes in it and had oatmeal for breakfast. Don't care.

Helping with Homework

I think homework for kids in elementary school is ridiculous. There, I said it. I don't think that kids before sixth grade need to be taking schoolwork home.

I really want my kids to love learning, to develop study skills, and to succeed in school. But I don't want them to have homework in elementary school. I feel like people generally hold the belief that there is a value to the way homework develops study habits. But I was a little shocked (and relieved?) to learn that there is solid research that says that homework in the early grades does not actually determine study skills for later grades. It is not indicative of learning or progress and does not teach kids anything other than burnout.

The average elementary school day is seven hours. Developmentally, kids in elementary school should not be required to spend more than seven hours on schoolwork. They need to be playing at this age, too, which is also a *huge* part of cognitive development. When kids go to school until three and then spend their evenings doing worksheets, we are squashing the time that they actually need to work on other developmental tasks.

In addition, at this age, homework is very rarely self-directed or independent. It becomes a responsibility for the parent, and places a burden on family life. When I pick my younger kids up, I want it to be family time. And I want there to be time for them to be involved in enriching activities like music lessons or sports. I hear so many friends talk about how the nightly homework takes up a big portion of their evening. I hated this fight.

When my kids started getting loads of homework at ages six and seven, initially I fought back. I did my research and found advocacy groups of other parents who were opting out. I took letters in to the teachers and explained that we would not be doing schoolwork at home. I hated being "that mom." I am a people-pleaser and I worried about what the teachers thought of me. But sanity at home was more important.

Eventually, I actually ended up moving my kids to a local magnet school that had a no-homework policy outside of practicing math facts and reading. No worksheets, no drama at night. It was blissful. And guess what? That school outperforms the test scores of most others in the district, even without homework. I am also pleased to report that when my oldest went to junior high and had to develop homework habits, *it was not that hard*. He did not need seven years of ruined evenings to ramp up to being able to do homework in middle school. He just needed to be an age when that level of responsibility was developmentally appropriate.

Once it starts, homework is not my responsibility. I'll inquire about it occasionally but remembering to do it, deciding when to do it, that is up to my kids. I have some minimum standards for grades. They don't have to be perfect. There are consequences for grades that fall way below ability. But I'm not holding their hands to make the grade on a daily basis.

Pinterest-Worthy Birthday Parties

Our birthday parties are more of a "glorified playdate." We have a pool. Maybe there is a sleepover. At this point, the kids make cupcakes for their siblings. We have a "donut wall" that India made of plywood and dowel rods that gets reused at each birthday party with cheap donuts from the grocery store and that's all the "wow factor" I can offer.

Making Lunches

Nope. Hate it. Not doing it. They can all buy lunch. Luckily our school district has a pretty healthy menu, but I'd be buying it even if they didn't just to avoid the task because IT IS THE WORST.

Fighting the Picky Eaters

I fought this battle for a long time. I really did. We had showdowns at the table over taking one small bite of a green bean.

We had crying and gagging and lots of drama. I finally conceded. I will not spend my time making a kid eat something they don't like, but I will also not be a short-order cook. I have two amazing eaters who are game for anything, and two kids who are on the Beige Diet. I raised them all the same, and just have to accept that some kids are biologically picky. So I have a limited alternative meal for them on hand. At the beginning of the week I make a big batch of brown rice in the rice-cooker. I then put that whole pot right into the fridge. If they don't like what I'm serving they can heat up some rice, heat up some canned beans, and eat carrots from the fridge. It gets them a decently healthy meal of things on their acceptable list of foods, and I don't have to make it.

My Kids Excelling at Anything

My kids aren't insanely good at anything. They are exceedingly average at a number of things. Maybe even above average. But none of them are prodigies. And I'm okay with it.

When children are small, doing everything "perfectly" tends to center around domesticity. Making homemade baby food, doing the most with crafts, having a perfectly kept home. But when kids get a little older, it becomes about activities. Sports, performing arts, orchestra, pick your poison. But there is a ton of pressure to figure out the thing your kid is going to do well, and then make them amazing at it, at an age well before they really have the agency to choose their own passions.

I am constantly befuddled as to what extracurricular activities I should have my kids involved in. Just figuring out the timing of classes and game schedules is enough to make me want to take a nap, but I also second-guess what activities would be best for each kid in terms of their natural abilities and talents versus what I really want for them. I've watched kids cry while being forced out onto a baseball field. I wanted my kids to come to their own interests naturally.

I've also seen kids who are legit passionate about something, and then that something takes over family life. I have friends who spend every afternoon at the dance studio, or whose weekends involve traveling with a sports team. I have family members whose children have missed every one of my kids' birthdays in favor of soccer. I knew that's not what I wanted. It also didn't seem to be what my kids wanted. None of them were begging to be more involved in activities than they already were.

I've been really low-key about activities with my kids. I've been chided that my boys might not be able to "compete" in high school if they were not doing club sports in elementary. But I didn't want that level of intensity about sports in our lives at that age, especially when there is no guarantee they will be interested in that sport later in life. And even if they were, I just wasn't willing to put the time in as some kind of "best athlete" insurance policy. They have played a number of sports casually throughout their younger years, always in settings with minimal practices and games, and never year-round, and I have no regrets. One kid went on to play a sport in middle school, and then quit. He's now entering high school playing a totally different sport.

My girls have both played a few sports, but were not very interested. When they were little I had them try all kinds of things from karate to baseball to dance. The thing that seems to have stuck is theater. But this is yet another area where I've had parents warn me that I need to up our game. "You've got to have them in dance, too, if you want them to be a triple threat." "You've got to get them into community theater to build their résumé." Again, I've opted to take a casual approach instead. They've taken a handful of dance classes. We don't do community theater because it's just too intense at this age. They take a weekly class at a local regional theater that culminates in an end-of-year performance, and they do an annual play at their school, and that's our commitment for now.

I value seasons of time without my kids in many activities. We've had seasons of sports playoffs and intense theater tech weeks: the harried evenings, the dinners eaten in the car or on the field. With four kids all in different activities, life can quickly be sabotaged by nightly practices or rehearsal and weekend shows and games. I've throttled it all back and I am loving it. We eat dinner together every night and it isn't from a drive-thru. We have time for homework. We have time to just sit around and talk, or play a game. We are not stressed or overscheduled. I know there is a lot to be learned from group sports or lessons but I also think there is a lot to be learned from being present in an unharried season of family life. Learning how to just "be." Learning to value slow dinners and long conversations and really connecting and being vulnerable with your family. I want my kids to be able to explore their passions and we will certainly have seasons where activities and sports will ramp up. But I'm compelled to push back against the cultural norm of sports over family life. It's been really beautiful to have a season where our family time is the priority.

Opting out is the new overscheduled.

CHEERLEADERS AND ASS-KICKERS

The typical expression of opening Friendship would be something like, "What? You too? I thought I was the only one!"

C. S. LEWIS

I had always imagined I would experience motherhood in tandem with a community of other women. But somehow, in my early days of motherhood, I found myself completely without a community.

Prior to starting our family we had been a part of the same church plant for fifteen years. I sang on the worship team and led the global missions ministry. My husband was a staff pastor. All of our friends were people we'd met at the church, and most of them were on staff or on the elder board. To say we lived in a bubble would be an understatement.

In the aftermath of the miscarriages and adoption drama, I started feeling uneasy with our church. For one, the more I got involved in activism around social justice, the more uncomfortable I became with some of the church's philosophies around missions and even orphan care. I had read Steve Corbett and Brian Fikkert's *When Helping Hurts,* and I was beginning to see how some of our well-intended practices as a church were steeped in a lack of understanding of the needs of the people we were trying to serve. At the time, I was the lead volunteer on the African missions branch of our church. Twice, I had led teams on mission trips to Zimbabwe that, in retrospect, were very problematic. Now I was learning about the issues inherent in short-term mission trips, from the way they patronize the poor to the misuse of funds involved in sending a team of twenty people to a remote location instead of funding the people already on the ground. I had also been part of a team that visited an "orphanage" our church built in India that housed hundreds of kids with living parents. And I was learning about the problems of "orphanages" that essentially entice children away from impoverished but living parents, spending money to clothe and feed kids separate from their families when that money could be used to help keep families together.

Around the same time, my views were shifting on issues like women's roles, LGBT inclusion, and politics. I was vocal about these shifting ideas, because . . . well, because that's who I am. I was loudly critical when a friend was asked to "step down" from church leadership because he was gay. I asked questions about the yearly budget, about why more money was spent on full-color glossy handouts and Easter marketing signs than on helping the poor in our community. I pointed out the lack of diversity on the church staff when a third of our town's population was Mexican. When the wife of an elder sent an email forward about Obama being the literal anti-Christ to every elder and pastor of the church and I was the only person who seemed to mind, I knew that things were bad.

Basically, I was becoming a pain in everyone's ass. In Christian communities, when people start bucking the system, it's easy to attribute their opposition to a church's leadership to one of the three *S*'s: sinfulness, secular ideology, or a slippery slope. For many, my sudden desire to debate these ideas was a sign that I was losing my faith. Their reaction only infuriated me even more, because I felt that I was drawing closer to *Jesus's actual teachings.*

I was still going to the weekly moms' group, but the discussions felt tone-deaf. I was worried about topics that felt a bit weightier than whether or not I was remembering to apply lipstick before my husband got home or whether or not I had my "quiet time." Like, why am I discussing my morning routine when what I am really dealing with is my son turning two while still living at an orphanage, or the fact that I just had another miscarriage, or that I have mastitis from breastfeeding, am experiencing panic attacks and intrusive thoughts, and also maybe my marriage is really bad.

I wasn't a special snowflake whose problems were bigger than anyone else's. As we went around the circle, I had some close friends that I knew were also holding back. A dying parent, a husband with a brain tumor, a child with a new and difficult diagnosis. But our conversation prompts were based on Christian culture prescriptions, not on vulnerability. Week after week, we talked about fluff when I knew a lot of us at that circle were in real pain. So I started to point this out. Why are we even here, if we aren't talking about the real stuff?

I could have been more patient. I was shifting my views on many things that I used to believe, and I wanted everyone to be on board. I felt like a big veil had been lifted. So many things that I believed to be true of Christianity, I was beginning to understand were influenced by other forces. I felt like I had been deceived, and I was digging for the truth at every turn, questioning everything and wanting the people close to me to come along for the ride.

In short, I was obnoxious and self-righteous and sure that I was right. Those are not fun traits in a friend.

My friendships were shifting and then, shortly after Kembe came home and we were adjusting to life with four kids, my husband was "released" from his position at church. If you are not familiar with the inner workings of churches, very rarely is someone fired. We use Christian-speak like "released" or "blessed into a new ministry" or "called out to a new vocation" because it sounds better, and because we don't want to be held responsible for actions that could reflect poorly on us.

This kind of code-speak is rife in Christian circles, and it can range from annoying to downright toxic. Christians can rely on God-speak to distance themselves from personal responsibility or owning their own decisions, and they can also use it to avoid vulnerability. You can blame anything on a prompting from God, from skipping out on a commitment to breaking up with someone. Here's a short glossary of other church terms:

WHAT THEY SAID	WHAT THEY MEAN
God put it on my heart . . .	I'm going to give you unsolicited advice right now.
I'm just gonna let the spirit lead.	I did not prepare for this.
We're just gonna love on people.	We have no tangible way to help people on this mission trip.
How can I pray for your sister specifically?	Please give me the dirt on your sister.
I'm going to pray about that.	The answer is no.
I'm not in that season of life right now.	The answer is no.
I don't feel led in that direction.	The answer is no.
That's not my spiritual gift.	The answer is no.
You're creating a stumbling block.	I'm objectifying you but I'm gonna blame you for it.
Bless her heart.	Sucks to be her.
Grace covers me.	I don't want to own my bad behavior.
Have faith when you sow and God will return it unto you in seven folds.	Give me your money.
Let go, and let God.	I'm gonna minimize your genuine concern and shame you for having situationally appropriate anxiety.
Hate the sin, love the sinner.	I'm uncomfortable with gay people.
God doesn't call the equipped, He equips the called.	I don't want to take the time to learn about this.
I'll pray for you.	I want you to think I'm doing something helpful without actually having to do anything.
We missed you at church.	We are judging you.
Pray more, worry less/faith over fear/lift it up.	Get over it.
I'm guarding my heart.	I don't want to go out with you.
Fellowship	What the rest of the world calls "eating."
Doing life together	Eating together a lot.
I don't see his fruit.	I like to use biblical metaphors when I judge others.
Lord willing	I have no intention of doing this but I don't want to be direct about it.
We feel called in a different direction.	I'm making a call that you can't question because, Jesus.
We're always looking for help with the children's ministry.	Know your place, woman.

"God's will" can become a cover for all manner of bad behavior, from little slights and rejections to outright evil. This is accepted in certain Christian circles, whether it's simply passive-aggressive or veering into spiritual abuse, because we've been trained that we cannot question God. When we present as if all of our actions and decisions are the responsibility of an omnipotent God, as if our will had nothing to do with it, we disallow the people we love to have feelings or concerns about what we are doing. It's lacking in empathy when we do something that can be hurtful or disappointing to another person and then point to God and shrug, as if we can't help it and can't own it. But we need to be able to question human decisions. And we need to call on each other to be more direct, more honest, and more accountable with the words we use. They matter.

Anyway, after my husband was "not-fired," continuing to attend this church became untenable. We decided it was time to move on. When we did, it felt like we walked away from the only community of friends I had known for the past fifteen years. Sure, I had been frustrated with them at times, but these were the people who had walked with us through many hardships. They were not bad people. But I had underestimated how much "doing church" together was the glue for these relationships. When my family stepped away from the rhythms of being heavily involved in the church, we also stepped out of that community of friends.

Outside of that church community I had no idea how to start making friends. As an introvert I am terrible at small talk. I'm much more comfortable talking about deeper issues than about the weather or how the soccer team is doing this season. I have the uncomfortable-for-others tendency of going *way* too deep in conversations with strangers as an attempt to avoid the chitchat and get to something meaningful. For example, at school pickup:

Oh, hi. You must be Bella's mom. [awkward pause] So what do you think happens when we die?

It doesn't help that I struggle with insecurity. After social situations with people outside my inner circle, I tend to replay every interaction over and over to try to figure out how I was perceived. It is not uncommon for me to lie awake for hours after a party, rehashing every conversation I had, and berating myself for where I went wrong in each situation.

I think this is why I was drawn to blogging. Despite my anxieties, I am still a social person. I do desire connection and community. Blogging allows me to communicate without all the baggage of social anxiety that burdens me in real life. But the blogging was a double-edged sword. In part, because it's a false sense of intimacy. It doesn't really replace the experience of in-person relationships. In addition, blogging allows me to present a version of myself that I can't always replicate in person. The result is that many people feel that they know me, but in person I am overwhelmed with the fear that I will disappoint and that I won't be able to be as funny or composed or personable as I am online. It turns out I am more comfortable communicating through a computer screen than in a room with someone.

Still, the Internet was the one place I had success in making new friends. I found other women whose families looked like mine. I found other people who shared my faith, and held a similar approach to how that faith should be lived out. I found friends who were bold and irreverent and loved Jesus but maybe cussed a little. I found women who were okay being authentic and transparent and messy. It made me feel so much less lonely to be able to read and comment on the blogs of like-minded women.

But in my daily life, I was incredibly isolated. Midway through Jafta's kindergarten year, I realized I did not have the phone number of a single other parent at his school. I had no one to call and ask if tomorrow was early dismissal, or if they could pick him up in a pinch. I had few real-life friends to go to coffee with or see a movie with or have over for wine and a good cry. I didn't have a mothers' circle of friends, and I was crushed that I found myself so alone.

I spent a couple of years in that lonely state, with friendships being one of the biggest pain points in my life. It was a weird stage of life because at the time, my blog was read by thousands of women a day, many of whom would make comments like, "We would totally be friends in real life!" Those comments stung, because I was ashamed of not having friends in real life. I finally decided I needed to set friend goals. It just wasn't going to come naturally so I was going to have to be proactive and work at it. First, I had to identify *who*. I took inventory of the women I had met online, and I decided to do something bold. I did the friendship equivalent of asking them out.

There was Jamie, who was a missionary in Costa Rica. We connected on our philosophies of missions and general cynicism. There was Jen, a blogger from Texas, and Tara, a midwife in Haiti who I'd met while adopting Kembe. They both had big transracial families and shared my love of sarcasm. There was Sarah B, who edited a progressive Christian magazine I wrote for, and who was one of the smartest women I knew. There was Sarah G, who I shared a mutual friend with, and who moved to Peru to start a nonprofit just as we were becoming friends. These were women I really clicked with and wanted to get to know better. But four of the six of us lived in different countries. It seemed an unlikely way to form a community, but I decided to try it anyway. I sent a very vulnerable (and in retrospect, somewhat cringey) letter to each of them, and to about six other women as well, and basically said this:

> I am kind of sucking at maintaining relationships right now. I have been thinking of trying to create a group of female friends. I want somewhere where I can share that I'm not feeling balanced or I'm scared I'm failing as a mom or I'm too tired to have sex with my husband or I don't know if I even want to attend church . . . all that heavy stuff. But I also want to laugh with people I love and basically just be in community. And realistically, for me, that's probably going to happen online more than in real life right now. Would you be interested in trying something like this?

Of the eleven women I sent the letter to, some said no. Whether they were too busy or not interested or didn't actually want to go deep or just didn't like me, who knows. Like in dating, rejection is inherent when you are making friends. But six of us put our hands together and said yes, let's do this. Let's go all in. Let's bring our sarcasm and our hope, our ugly parts and our hopeful parts, our faith and our doubts, and let's go deep.

The six of us slowly built our friendship. We started meeting yearly. We tested the waters of how deep we could go with each other. By year two, our group became a safe space where we knew we could say *anything* to each other. And we did. We walked each other through devastations and divorces, parenting challenges and personal triumphs. We don't always agree. We hold strong and sometimes differing views of God and faith. We let that be okay. We like to say we are equal parts cheerleaders and ass-kickers to each other. It's a space where one of us can pop in and say, "Is my thinking clear on this?" and that might be met with, "Girl, totally. You are the smartest," but it also might be met with, "You sound irrational. Go take a nap."

It felt like an embarrassment of riches. I had gone from being adrift and friendless to being enveloped by a warm and loving circle of women. Sometimes you find friends you laugh with. You share the same brand of humor and you cackle with each other until someone has to run to the bathroom. You mock as a love language. You talk in GIFs. You giggle until your cheeks hurt. Sometimes you find friends you bond with emotionally. You pull off your mask and expose your ugly parts and they see it all and say, "Okay. I love you." You tell them your deepest secrets and feel known. Sometimes you find friends you click with intellectually. You debate and analyze and ponder life's mysteries. You share book recommendations and articles and ideas. You feel smarter for knowing them. Sometimes you find friends you work well with. You inhabit similar spaces and push each other to be better at the things you do. You talk shop and strategize and share resources. You edit and whiteboard and dream and support career trajectories. Sometimes you find friends who share your passion for justice. Your shared vision for a better world solidifies your bond. You get angry together. You plan together. You learn together. Sometimes, the rarest of times, you find all of these things in the same group of friends and you could just cry that you get to be lifted up, in your dark times and in your triumphs, by such an amazing sisterhood.

These girls have seen me through my blackest days, and I'm so grateful to them. But if you are reading this book and feeling a pang of isolation at not having good friendships, I am here to testify that I see you. I've been there. And I'm certain if you put yourself out there enough, you can create your own community.

It might be awkward at first, and it might not look the way you thought your community would look. Like so many things in life, it takes intention and work. But it will be worth it.

Thankfully, I was able to build a similar circle of friends in my own community, too. I also achieved this by taking risks, stumbling, and working hard to make it happen. I really wanted to develop a group of mom friends at my kids' school and was striking out with just letting it happen organically. So I decided, one year, that I would host a back-to-school mimosa party for moms on the first day of school. I figured that having a party around kids going back to school was one way to find "my people." I invited, basically, *anyone* from the kids' school. About thirty moms showed up. The crowd died down about an hour in, and there was a smaller group of us left, still engrossed in a rather frank conversation about motherhood. One of them said, "I'm so glad you did this. I didn't know there were other moms like me at the school. You know. *Other moms that hate everyone.*" We all nodded and knew exactly what she meant. None of us actually hate everyone, of course. But we were the group of moms with maybe a touch more introversion and sarcasm than other moms. We felt on the fray, and overwhelmed at the idea of putting ourselves out there. That day we found each other.

I kept inviting these women. Hosting is my love language, but it's also a great way to make friends. I invited them to *Bachelor*-watching nights, to local concerts, to parties with the kids. And from there, another community emerged. I'm happy to report that I now have an amazing group of mom friends at the kids' school—women who love my kids, who vacation with us, and who are happy to come over to my house in their pajamas with a bottle of prosecco to watch trashy TV or do face masks.

Relationships at any age take work, but when you've got a lot of kids, and you aren't plugged in to a church or a built-in community from your occupational or academic circumstances, it can feel absolutely impossible. I found myself nearly friendless at one of the loneliest times of my life, and I'm so glad I pushed back my feelings of mortification, put myself out there, and found some friends to "go steady" with me.

SHAKEN

I have seen many storms in my life. Most storms have caught me by surprise, so I had to learn very quickly to look further and understand that I am not capable of controlling the weather, to exercise the art of patience and to respect the fury of nature.

PAULO COELHO

When I decided to adopt from Haiti, I thought that adopting internationally would be less dramatic than what I'd been through before. With Jafta, I lived through three years of questions and ambiguity before being able to adopt him. I also lived through three years of infertility and miscarriages before having India. In 2006, when Jafta was almost two and India was six months old, we flew down to Haiti to meet our future son. I had no idea that it would take three years and an earthquake before he would come home.

When we first met with the director of the orphanage, we tried to give her a window into our family so that she could advise us on which waiting child was right for us. "We are a loud

family," I explained. "We are not wallflowers. I have two assertive kids who are not shy, and their sibling will need to be able
to keep up." "I know just the kid," she said. The orphanage director described Kembe as the loudest kid in the orphanage, and
she was right. He was assertive and bold and charming and
funny. Kembe seemed to match the personality of our family.
Then the director told us his birthday, and I gasped. It was the
exact same day and year as India's. I had to laugh, this would
make them the world's weirdest "twins." We said yes to the
match, and went home to wait for the paperwork to pass
through Haiti's department of family services. This was supposed to take about nine months.

Adoptions in Haiti were rife with corruption and arbitrary
delays. Our orphanage refused to pay bribes or grease palms.
And so our paperwork was pushed to the bottom of the pile,
over and over. That nine months passed, and then a year, and
then another.

We tried to visit Kembe as much as possible while we were
waiting, though each visit took its toll. It was always a relief to
see how well he was cared for. But no matter how well an orphanage is run, it's still an orphanage. A rotating door of caregivers, even amazing ones, is not a replacement for the love and
attention of a family.

While we pined for him and absolutely thought of him as our
son, he was living his life in Haiti, oblivious to us. He knew us as
people who visited, but he did not (appropriately so, given the
situation) view us as his parents. He wasn't jumping into our
arms when we arrived. We showed up enthusiastic and excited
to see him, and he wanted nothing to do with us. I knew that
this was a GOOD THING. It showed he was bonded to his
nanny. It showed he discriminated to whom he gave affection.
As a therapist, I could step out of my feelings and look at it clin-

ically and say, these are signs of a child with a solidly formed attachment to his caregivers. But as a mom, it broke my heart. Each time we visited, it took him a long time to warm up to us. We would take him to dinner with us, and he would be sad and unresponsive all evening. But then we would take him back to the orphanage, and he would run around hugging every kid several times, and seemed like the happy, engaging boy we had heard about. I wanted him to be that boy with us.

Each visit was also a tangible reminder of how much he was growing up without us. As the years went on and Kembe got to know us, he started to become comfortable with us. By the time he was two, he was fun and engaging during our visits. He would run to us when we showed up and want to be held all day. We got to see the little comedian we'd heard about. But then he would get upset when we set him down, or when we left for our hotel for the night. He would be watching for any sign we were going to leave, and then he would cry and cry, which in turn would make me bawl. When our trips were over, the goodbyes were incredibly painful for all of us. I desperately wanted to bring him home.

During the years we waited, it was impossible not to think of him every single day. I would be at the grocery store, or out with friends, and would think, *I have a child who doesn't live with me.* I had believed that things with Jafta had been uniquely challenging because we were living as a family during the time of uncertainty. But with Kembe, I realized that having a child living in an orphanage during the uncertainty was not a better option. Once again, I found myself having to let go of outcomes and live in ambiguity during the process of bringing a child into our family.

As time went on, our visits increased. By the last year of our wait, my husband and I tried to make sure one of us was down there every three to four months, just to check on paperwork. In January of 2010, I took a quick trip down to make sure everything was moving along. It had now been three long years since we met Kembe. I had given birth to Karis in that time and I was still nursing her, so I decided to take her with me on this trip.

On our second night in Haiti, Kembe was playing with a friend in the front yard of the guesthouse where we were staying. Karis was sleeping in a car carrier. At one point, I went inside to get my purse from an upstairs room. On the way down the stairs, the house started shaking violently. It was shaking so hard that I had to grab on to the railing to make it down. The ground was pitching and tiles were flying off the walls. I could see cracks forming in the walls, and it was difficult to see and even to walk because it felt like I was being thrown from side to side. The sound was like the roar of a helicopter landing on the roof of the house. I made it down the stairs, ran to grab the car seat holding Karis, and then ran outside to find Kembe. He was startled and crying. I grabbed Kembe and Karis into my lap and held them tight. We sat in the middle of the yard as the shaking continued. People were screaming. Though it lasted only a few minutes, it felt like an eternity. The people in the streets were panicking, and we saw two women in towels, who must have run from the shower.

It's startling what goes through your mind at a time like that. My first thought was keeping the kids safe, which I instinctively knew would be outside. I tried to position us as far from anything that could fall as I could. I was also trying to figure out what was going on. The shaking and noise were so extreme that I thought for sure it could not be an earthquake. I had never heard of Haiti being hit with an earthquake, so I assumed something else was going on. I thought maybe the island was being bombed. I also had some thoughts about Armageddon. It felt like I was dropped into a disaster movie. I thought the ground might open. Mostly, I knew that it was bad, and I was very scared. The pendant lights in the house were swinging, and one smashed to the ground. The kitchen cabinets lost all their contents, and there was glass everywhere. Dressers, lamps, and pictures slid and collided across the floor. A table collapsed.

Once the shaking stopped, those of us staying in the house gathered and made sure everyone was okay. Luckily, we were. About ten minutes later, there was another earthquake. This was not as bad as the first, but still worse than any I've been through. Again, I grabbed the kids and sat us down in the middle of the yard. These aftershocks continued for hours. I'm told at least thirteen of them measured above a 4.0. It felt like they were coming every twenty or thirty minutes for a while. We were all pretty traumatized by the first quake, and the continued shocks were extremely stressful. I tried to compose myself so that I wouldn't freak out the kids any further, but I was fighting back tears with each new tremor, and wondering when it would stop and how we would get through the night. Or even the next minute.

I decided to head over to my friend Tara's house, who thankfully lived walking distance from where I was staying. Tara was a midwife in Haiti with the same organization that ran Kembe's orphanage, and had become a good friend over the years. Like most families I passed by on my walk to her house, hers was gathered in the driveway. We sat outside together for a long time, with our kids gathered around us, and I was grateful for their company as more aftershocks came. As the night turned into the next day, we began to comprehend the extent of devastation, and how fortunate we had been. Tara's husband, Troy, went out several times to check on others. He saw hillside neighborhoods where every house had buckled. In others, houses had caved in. Bodies lining the streets. People were walking by with grave injuries and no hope of finding medical aid. It was mass chaos.

That first night I was sure I was going to die in an aftershock. I thought Karis and Kembe were going to die. I cried, thinking of the two kids I'd left at home who would go through life without a mom or their siblings. I thought I'd never see my husband again. My anxiety was consuming my every thought.

In the hours just after the earthquake, we had a brief interlude of Internet access via satellite. Troy was able to post to his Twitter account that there had been an earthquake, and that he and his family were okay. As information became available, he posted about the people he knew who had survived, and about the stories he was hearing of the devastation reported by the friends who were stopping by. We really had no idea of the scope of this earthquake, though each visitor brought more and more troubling information.

At some point in the evening, the orphanage staff stopped by to report that all of the kids were okay, which was a huge relief. But later, a woman who ran another orphanage in Haiti came by and informed us that the government office that contained the adoption paperwork for every child waiting to be adopted in Haiti had crumbled. She was in tears, questioning what would happen to the kids like Kembe who had been waiting years to go to their families. In a place like Haiti, a hurdle like this could mean all progress came to a screeching halt. I felt the panic of a fresh consequence of this earthquake to agonize over.

When the Internet finally came back on, we all quickly grabbed our laptops, hoping to send a few emails, find out when flights were resuming, and log onto CNN to see if we could get a broader view of what was happening in Port-au-Prince. I'll never forget Tara finding a picture of the crushed presidential palace, and the dread that came over the room when she showed us. And then hearing Troy realize that his tweets were being broadcast from every major news network. There were no reporters in Haiti yet, and no flights coming in or out. Troy was the news. He was not just updating our friends and family. He was updating the world.

I logged onto Facebook. What I saw brought me to tears. All of my friends were posting messages for me—my wall was full of people asking about me, offering to help, and posting their prayers of support. My husband had updated my blog for me, which received hundreds of comments that first day. Even though our Internet connection was brief, I opened my blog comments and continued to read them after we lost connection—a way of feeling support in the glow of my laptop after our contact was cut off. I sat reading my Facebook and blog comments long into the night, bawling and feeling bolstered by the prayers and support of friends and strangers. It was one of the lowest points in my life—but it was also the moment when I felt some of the most intense love from others.

The days that followed brought a different kind of terror, a dull, overwhelming sense of dread. It was a cloudy, dissociative feeling, in contrast to the sharp terror of the earthquake itself.

All I wanted was to get out of Haiti and be reunited with my family, but the last thing I wanted was to leave Kembe in the middle of this natural disaster. I'd heard reports that it might be weeks or even months before the airports reopened. We began to fear robbery, riots, and mass illness. Karis had developed a mystery fever. I was in a crippled country with no infrastructure in a state of international emergency with a sick baby and a shell-shocked little boy who should have been mine by now but wasn't.

I'm a "doer." In moments of crisis I like to spring into action, to problem-solve and help those around. But there was nothing in this situation that I could control. I was parenting two small kids so I couldn't venture out and try to help the wounded like Troy and Tara were doing. I was unable to do anything but focus on the best next move for my family.

Karis's fever persisted and there was no medical care available for her. After several sleepless nights with a sick baby I knew I had to get her home. At the urging of the U.S. government we made our way to the U.S. embassy. It was the only way out of the country, but it meant leaving Kembe behind at the orphanage. When we arrived at the orphanage to drop Kembe off, the children and staff were sleeping in the driveway, unprotected behind a toppled gate. I was so afraid for him, but without his visa completed I couldn't take him with me. There was nothing we could do. Karis and I staying meant we would be a drain on resources in a struggling country. I couldn't help, and knew I needed to get Karis home. That was the hardest goodbye I've ever had to say. I hugged him tight but tried to hide my tears. He was, thankfully, distracted by his reunion with his friends. He was happy to be with them again and excited at the adventure of an outdoor slumber party. He was, thankfully, young enough to be oblivious to the ongoing stressors the earthquake left behind.

When we arrived at the embassy, I let myself exhale for the first time since the earthquake. It was so comforting to walk through those stable walls. I think in the prior days I'd only slept about two hours each night. I was more tired than I'd ever been in my life. The shaking continued, but we were sheltered. The

embassy fed us MREs every four hours and gave us regular updates about how we might get home. Once again I found myself
sleeping under the stars, this time because the building was so
full. There were hundreds of us sleeping on the embassy lawn
that night, lined up on blankets on the grass.

The next day, military planes arrived and began to fly people
out in groups. No one knew where they were going, passengers
didn't learn the destination airport until they were in the air
because decisions were being made in real time. No one cared,
we were bound for somewhere in the United States, and we were
relieved. When my group was next, staff told us the protocol for
boarding the plane. We were to leave behind any suitcases. Each
person could bring along one small personal item, like a backpack or a purse, *unless* they had a baby. "Your baby or your bag,"
they said. I had a baby, a sick one. And a diaper bag full of things
I needed for said baby. I also had a suitcase, a car seat, and a
stroller, but those were all left at the embassy. Along with Karis,
I was also accompanying Tara's children back to the States. Troy
and Tara were staying on, setting up a makeshift hospital and
administering care to the wounded because hospitals were
bursting at the seams. One of their kids generously carried my
diaper bag on for me, as I carried Karis in my arms.

They loaded us onto a military C-17. It flew in full of medical
volunteers, and it flew home a group of scared Americans. It
wasn't like any plane I'd ever been in. It was more like a cargo
carrier, with plastic jump seats along the edges facing inward
that we were directed to sit in. There was a pile of supplies and
boxes in the center of the plane. Everyone looked exhausted and
traumatized. Some had visible wounds. Many on the plane were
grieving people they had lost. We all diverted our eyes when
people on the plane could no longer hold in their grief, and
wailed or sobbed. We were all traumatized in some way. An

American military officer who was clearly not proficient in giving airline safety drills attempted to give us instructions on what to do in case of emergency. Only his wording was just a little off.

"Okay, uh . . . when the plane loses oxygen, you're gonna use that oxygen mask from under your seat. When the plane crashes into water, you're gonna use your seat to float. When the plane catches fire, you can use the parachutes along the wall. When the plane approaches a crash . . ." As he was explaining all of this in "when" instead of "if" language, every one of us was just staring at the others in horror. Pro-tip: Words matter when talking to a traumatized group of people who just survived a natural disaster.

At some point, we learned we were headed to a military base in Pennsylvania where the Red Cross was waiting for us with food, clothing, and a bank of phones to call our families and arrange our next flight. From there we were bused to a normal airport to fly home. As I walked through the airport, it seemed like every TV screen was tuned in to Haiti, even though it had been several days since the earthquake. It was surreal to watch reporters speaking from where I'd just been and to see Haiti getting so much international attention.

I was a wreck. I was in the same clothes I'd been wearing for four days, unshowered, not wearing a bra, and tired to the bone. I remember waiting for the commercial flight, surrounded by regular, non-traumatized passengers, feeling self-conscious about my greasy hair and disheveled appearance, holding a baby who also clearly needed a bath. As I walked onto the plane, a flight attendant announced that they had an earthquake survivor on board. The whole plane clapped for me, and I lost it. I didn't feel deserving. I could not stop thinking of all of the people who didn't have the luxury of being flown away, and who had lost so much that week.

I was grateful to be met at my local airport by my family and a number of friends. It has never felt so good to come home. I went home and slept for ten hours. When I woke up I didn't know how to move on from what had happened, and I didn't know how to cope with Kembe being in a devastated country. I called my best friend in tears because I didn't have a nursing bra to wear (mine were left in the suitcase in Haiti) and because I couldn't drive without a car seat (which was also left in Haiti) to get to Target to get a new bra. (*Don't judge me on the bra. I took it off because I was hunkering down for a good night's sleep out on the lawn of the embassy. Little did I know I would be braless for the next eighteen hours.*) Really, I was crying about the earthquake and the stress and missing my son and how tired I was and for the trauma of what had happened to everyone in Haiti that week. But these were the things that seemed insurmountable in the moment. The bra. I was crying about a bra.

The day after returning from Haiti was a blur of watching the news in Haiti, and scouring the Internet for updates about the adoption process. That night we turned on Diane Sawyer, as there was a murmur that she had visited our son's orphanage. They showed footage of the children, sleeping in the driveway for fear of going back into a house that could topple. They also showed footage of the kids during the day, happy and playing. And then suddenly, she picked up one of the kids. It was Kembe. I can't express how that felt—just being able to see his face and know that he was okay.

I left Haiti assuming that Kembe's adoption was stalled. When I got home, someone I didn't even know had sent me a message through Facebook. She asked me to get involved in petitioning the government to grant humanitarian parole to orphans who had been matched with approved families. It was estimated that the earthquake created thousands of orphans, who needed shelter and care. Yet there were many children sitting in orphanages who had parents who had already passed through every stage of approval to adopt and were simply waiting on signatures and visas. We were petitioning both governments to expedite those specific children to go home to their families, both to ensure their safety and to create space in orphanages for the children who recently lost parents.

I penned a frantic blog post that first night home—asking people to call our state reps. I asked my Facebook friends to do the same. They posted my blog as their own status update. I watched the word get out quickly. The next morning, I woke up to messages on my cellphone from my local congressman as well as Senator Barbara Boxer's office. Before I had even had a chance to call them, people had called on my behalf. My government leaders were aware of my story and working behind the scenes—all because of a blog post pleading for help.

A friend, who had been adopted internationally herself, decided to act as my press secretary and book me on as many talk shows as possible to speak on humanitarian parole. Haiti was still very much in the news and local channels were anxious to get an interview with the "local Orange County woman who survived the earthquake." It all seemed very overdramatic to me but I took the interviews because I wanted to use the attention to talk about getting these kids home. Five days later the U.S. secretary of state and the Haitian government agreed to give humanitarian parole to already-in-process orphans. Kembe was coming home.

I'm extremely humbled by the way my friends and readers moved into action. Generally I have a lot of ambivalence toward social networking. It sucks my time and spurs my FOMO. But I am so grateful that the moment I was in a pit of despair, a virtual mob of people put their hands together and collectively pulled me out.

Despite our joy at bringing Kembe home, there was also a lot of stress in the details. We'd made well-crafted plans for what our trip to get him would be like. Plans to stay in Haiti for a week and gradually acclimate him to being with us more each day before we left. Plans to have solid goodbyes with his nanny and friends. Instead, the kids were given very little notice, dressed in their best clothes, and shuttled to the airport in the dark of night. None of their nannies could accompany them. Kembe was evacuated on the same C-17 that I was evacuated on. I later saw a photo of Kembe being ushered onto the plane by a marine. I can't imagine what he must have been feeling.

They flew the kids to Florida, where my husband met Kembe at the airport. But first, they had to "process" the kids, which meant that all of the children had to sit in a holding cell for almost twelve hours as customs and immigration workers pored over their files. Finally, scared and traumatized, they were released to their parents. Then Kembe and his dad took another flight home to L.A., where the other kids and I were waiting. I don't think I've ever seen Jafta more excited. At this moment, I was grateful for all of those awkward trips we had taken to get to know him. We were not strangers. He knew and recognized all of us. He and the kids immediately started playing together. After all of the trauma, it was a happy moment for our family.

We got home and showed him around the house. He still spoke mostly Creole and we did our best to translate everything. "This is your bed." "This is your room." "This is where we play." Immediately, he and Jafta were in the backyard kicking a ball around.

I sat down, feeling I could truly rest for the first time since the earthquake. He was home. My son was home.

My four children came to me in very different ways, including two very different adoptions and two very different pregnancies. The process by which each child came into my life took something from me, and broke something inside me that maybe needed breaking. Each one was hard, and each one was so very worth it.

WHAT IS LOVE?
(BABY, DON'T HURT ME)

Compassion hurts. When you feel connected to everything, you also feel responsible for everything. You cannot turn away. Your destiny is bound with the destinies of others. You must either learn to carry the Universe or be crushed by it. You must grow strong enough to love the world, yet empty enough to sit down at the same table with its worst horrors.

ANDREW BOYD

O n occasion, I will hear people question whether or not adoptive parents love their adopted children as much as their biological children. Before I had adopted, this question offended me. OF COURSE THEY DO, I would tell myself, because thinking otherwise suggested some kind of biological determinism that made me uncomfortable. What kind of monster would favor their own genetics? Surely the human psyche is evolved enough to rise above biological favoritism. What are we, animals?

I do believe that adoptive parents can love all of their children equally. But I'm a little softer on that question now because adoption has taught me that love has many iterations, and requires so much more of us than I ever could have imagined. Adopting Jafta and almost losing him taught me to love without guarantees. I had to reach into the reserves of my own compassion and patience to do this. I had to abandon my own selfishness and find more love in myself than I'd ever thought imaginable. My next adoption was also a test of my ability to love. This time, I was challenged to love when that love was not reciprocated.

In Haitian Creole, there is a word, *degaje,* which basically means to "make it work." We were in serious *degaje* mode when Kembe first came home. I have always scoffed at the idea that there is any manual that can teach a mother how to do things the right way. When you are parenting four small children, one of whom speaks another language, there is NO MANUAL.

Our house was chaos. The inmates were running the asylum. Kembe brought a new energy to the house. It was big and wild and exuberant, and Jafta and India were totally eating it up. I kept wondering if it was all just a honeymoon phase, and if things were gonna come crashing down in a few days as their adrenaline wore off. (They did.) That first week, though, was joyful and manic and fun and TOTALLY FREAKING EX-HAUSTING. I had never been so proud of Jafta and India. Their welcoming generosity and tenderness to Kembe was enough to make me weep.

Kembe was also amazing with Karis, who was two years younger than him. There had been a number of younger children in his orphanage and he had often taken it upon himself to care for them, so he really liked playing big brother to her. He carried her around, held her hand as she tried to walk, and worked hard at getting a laugh from her.

When Kembe came home, Karis and I said goodbye to our nursing relationship. It became more and more difficult to find the space and time to sit still with Karis. I was distracted, and she was distracted. If we weren't in a quiet room, she was squirming and looking around and pretty much trying to order her milk "to go." Since the last time I was able to sit in a quiet room was *never*, nursing started to become a tug-of-war.

More than that, Kembe was grieving in those first few weeks. He vacillated between playing with abandon with his new siblings, and getting quiet and tearful. He missed his friends and his nannies, the only family he'd ever known. I needed my arms available. Karis was a happy baby who was content to sit and drink from a bottle as she interacted with the world. I knew that Kembe needed that spot on my lap.

So the week that Kembe came home, I cleaned out the bins that held my nursing covers. It was also the bin that held the receiving blankets, and the burp cloths and all the other items you use for a newborn. I folded them away with the bittersweet thought that I would never use these items again. I knew Karis would be our last baby. In my heart, but also because of a small surgical snip to my husband's nether regions that ensured it. I didn't want more children, but saying goodbye to the baby stage was just so profoundly sad for me. So much so that I sobbed to the point that my husband had to hide the children from their grief-stricken mother for a good fifteen minutes. I was grieving my baby growing up and overwhelmed that I had my new son home finally. There were so many emotions, but mostly, I was overcome with gratitude.

It was surreal to finally have Kembe in our home. Getting to know a three-year-old who is your son is wild. Kembe had a huge personality that in some ways reminded me of a little frat boy. He was silly and playful and extremely confident. He had skills with any kind of ball. He was loud and wildly energetic, a great match for Jafta. He thought that a bathtub full of water was the best thing ever. He wasn't so sure about grapes or ice cream or elevators. He was sweet and affectionate, and in the evenings he got a little homesick. He slept with a soccer ball, excited that for the first time in his life, something was not community property but actually *just his*. He squealed at the top of his lungs when he was happy. He had a million-watt smile and huge dimples, and we were absolutely smitten.

What none of us anticipated, though, was that Kembe did not share our hopes and dreams. He had not been pining for us. In fact, he wasn't pining for a family at all. It's a myth of the orphan trope that kids are sitting around the orphanages singing the "Maybe" song from *Annie*, dreaming of a future family. I think that may be true for some. But for a kid like Kembe, a family was not something he was even familiar with, so how could he be dreaming of it? Institutional life was all he knew. He had barely left the four walls of his orphanage for three years. He had no idea what family life looked and felt like. We disrupted *his* life in a big way. He was used to a rotating door of staff members and large-group living. And as one of the more assertive kids in the orphanage, he was also used to getting his way.

Adjusting to family life with two parents who are trying to connect with you in ways that are unfamiliar is not easy. Kembe pushed back hard. He was going to show us who was boss. (Spoiler alert: It was him.)

When he came home Kembe and India were both three. At this stage, whenever someone was cruel to India at school, she would come home and repeat whatever mean phrase she heard back to me, in an attempt to become the aggressor instead of the wounded. It made her feel some sense of power to take out the hurt by inflicting it on someone else. When India did it, it was usually something rather benign and silly that would make for a funny story later, when she was out of earshot. Some of her favorites included, "You're not the boss of me," or, "You aren't my friend anymore."

Kembe, on the other hand, was feeling out of control as he learned to live in a family. Much like India, his three-year-old self looked to the safe people in his life to experiment with power and aggression, and to repeat behaviors he had observed in the orphanage. The behaviors that resulted didn't make for funny stories. They were often a little horrifying, truthfully.

I want to pause and say that it's hard to recount this season, because Kembe today is so drastically different. It's hard to look at Kembe today, who is such a positive and encouraging sibling and son, and remember the journey it took for us to truly become a family, not just in name but in feeling. Because today, he's the kid most likely to send a text just telling me how awesome I am. He's the kid who gets recognized constantly at school for being a positive helper and example to younger kids. He's the kid who comes to me for advice with real-life problems, and tries to delay bedtime because he wants to stay up and talk with me.

It wasn't that way for a long time.

At a young age, living in a group environment with not enough caregivers, Kembe learned that there were two ways to get his needs met: to be the loudest/bossiest/most controlling, or to be the most hurt/helpless/needy. These behaviors are not unique to Kembe. They are quite common for children who have been institutionalized. These habits were developed because of a scarcity of attention and available arms in the orphanage, and formed because of the trauma of abandonment. His pain did not go away the second he had attentive parents. He did not know how to rest in the knowledge that an adult would meet his needs. He was hypervigilant. He was limbic. His behavior came from a place of fear, but on the surface—to a tired and very emotional parent struggling to stay in a place of compassion and connection—it looked like bids for control.

Kembe attended preschool three mornings a week and would play a game I called "purposeful pokeyness" when I picked him up. At his Montessori preschool, they had a rule that parents had to wait outside the windowed door to the classroom to pick up the kids. He did a half day there so when I picked him up, I would stand at the door to the class and wave to signal that it was time to go. Nine times out of ten, he would see me, and then *pretend not to see me,* and wait until all of the kids in the class saw me and started shouting for him to look. *Then,* he would walk as slowly as possible to the shoe area, and then pretend that he couldn't get his shoes on, and on and on and on with this dramatic game of slow motion (Can't find backpack! Shoe fell off! Have to go back to desk for forgotten item!) as I stood helplessly behind the door, waiting. And all the while, he would be stealing glances at me to see how I was going to respond. This kind of testing was pervasive in Kembe's interactions with me, and the preschool pickup is a very benign example of what was a consistent interactional pattern.

I tried my best to stay emotionally neutral with the preschool pickup dance, but on occasion I would lose my cool and chew him out as he walked out the door, which was fun because then all of the nearby parents would watch Kembe's face as he feigned confusion and assume that I was just a raving lunatic who gets mad at kids who struggle with their shoes. (And this is a whole other topic—the joys of other people assuming you are the meanest parent ever because they don't understand the dynamics of your kid's behavior.) Another behavior many institutionalized children display is seeking pity or positive attention from strangers while behaving in rejecting ways to parents.

This behavior went on well past his first year home. On the

first day of kindergarten, at a new school, I arrived in the car-pool line to pick up India and Kembe. Both of them clearly saw me pull up. India ran to the car gleefully. And Kembe pulled the same charade he pulled in preschool. He pretended he didn't see me, and three teachers had to call out to get him to acknowledge my presence. Then, he walked the most purposeful slow march I have ever seen. And you know what? I lost it. I lost it because I was stressed about picking up Jafta, whose school across town got out at the exact same time, but also I lost it because it had been a summer since I'd seen that behavior, and I was disappointed and hurt and not accessing my best empathy in that moment. So I called out the window in my "I mean business" voice:

"Huh-uh, Kembe. No way. We are not playing that game this year. Pick up the pace."

A teacher who was not paying attention to his slow-motion walk and just thought I was an impatient beyotch, looked at me with pursed lips and said,

"Hang on, Mom. He's coming."

But what her tone really said was,

"Take a chill pill, crazy lady."

I was embarrassed. And Kembe was smirking.

Side note: This is the point at which adoptive parents start to nod in recognition, while parents of typical kids interject that this is normal kid behavior that all kids engage in. And this is the point where I tell you: *NO*. It's not the same. It may happen on occasion, but it's not as purposeful and constant. This is a small example of behavior he displayed all day, every day. Being pokey at pickup was the tip of the iceberg.

To someone who doesn't understand attachment injury, it might look like manipulation. If you are a tired mom who is not able to always be mindful, it *feels* like manipulation. I had to actively work to remind myself that he was *four years old.* That he was not a mastermind bent on gaslighting me and making me crazy, but in fact a young and hurting child who needed love but who was also testing the limits of love out of fear.

And so again, I found myself at times asking myself, *What would a loving mother do right now?* What would a mother do if she was to love unconditionally, regardless of outcomes or reciprocation? What does love look like if I simply give it, and don't expect anything in return? What does love look like if it is completely independent of the way I feel I am being treated?

This is a lesson that all parents have to learn at some point. Sometimes our kids do not demonstrate the love back to us that we may have expected when we set out on this parenting journey.

I really had to come to terms with some of my own subconscious selfishness in learning to love Kembe the way he deserved to be loved. Of course I would never have directly thought, *I need my child to make me feel loved and give me emotional hits in order to love them back.* But I was surprised at what a challenge it was to freely give love when I felt like it was being withheld. So I loved "as if." I went through the motions until the feelings followed. I pushed in. I cuddled. I pursued. I resisted the urge to get riled up. And I reminded myself constantly that this was a former orphan who had lost everything, and this was all an expression of his grief. If I could stay in that mind-set, and not make it about myself or take it personally, I could maintain the empathy that Kembe deserved.

I loved Kembe relentlessly, and eventually, we bonded. His attachment injury began to heal. We began to experience the ease of a safe relationship. Many years later, I remember sitting by the sidelines of a soccer game when Kembe made an impressive goal. He did a little victory dance and then, in the middle of the game, he beelined over to me for a hug. As I watched him run back to the field while still smiling back at me, and I was welled up with the pride a parent feels for a child's success, I remember thinking how far we'd come. The story of the pre-school pickup, and the myriad of other behaviors that I will leave in the recesses of my memory, are so different from the warm and loving kid that Kembe is today. But even if that healing looked different, and even if those hard behaviors remained, loving unconditionally would have been the right thing to do.

I feel like each of my children has brought me great lessons around loving without fear, letting go of outcomes, and living with ambiguity. Loving Kembe taught me that love is not measured in positive moments or emotional strokes or ease of connection. Love is not measured by the number of warm fuzzy moments. Loving our children is not measured in how they make us feel. Those can all be outcomes of love, and I'm grateful to say that I've experienced those outcomes immeasurably with each one of my kids. But love is measured in worry, in effort, and in sacrifice, and in action. Love is a verb.

Do I love my adopted kids the same? Yes. I certainly do.

"SLEEP WHEN THE BABY SLEEPS" AND OTHER LIES

You know what it's like having a fourth kid? Imagine you're drowning, then someone hands you a baby.

JIM GAFFIGAN

I went from desperately wanting kids to having four kids in the course of four years. I didn't set out to have kids so close in age, but it's the way my family was formed.

Obviously, there are pros and cons to kids close in age. Now that the kids are older, I absolutely love it. They are passing through developmental stages together. The majority of years most of them are at the same school, and they enjoy the same things. We can all watch the same movies, I can put them in sports and activities together, and I'm not having to change diapers or chase a toddler while I am also in the "taxi driver" phase of life with teens.

I can also see that the Duggar family had a strategy that I

missed out on: having kids widely spaced enough that you have older kids taking care of the younger ones. None of my kids can ever "babysit" the others because they are practically peers. But I feel like for my personality, closely spaced kids is a real win.

Of course it didn't always feel like that. It was absolute chaos when the kids were younger. I am convinced that every baby book ever written was written by someone with only one child. Advice like "sleep when the baby sleeps" or "put your child on a sleep-eat-play schedule" does not really apply when you have four running around. "Wear your baby so your hands are free," they said.

I would love to see the advice book for parenting multiple small ones. It could have helpful tips like "how to pee while holding a baby" or "managing a toddler's time-out while breast-feeding a baby in a different room." I don't recall the solution to what happens if you are cooking and one child poops his diaper while another upends a box of Cheerios throughout the kitchen just as you need to remove something from the oven.

With four small kids, there is no right way to parent. You are just managing chaos. Every man for himself. He (or she) who cries loudest, wins. Nursing was the predictable time that all of the other children would stage a coup. They knew I was stuck, so that was their moment to scale the kitchen table and jump off, or draw on the wall with marker, or play "pool" with their dolls in the toilet.

Sleep at this point was a joke. We had three bedrooms and four kids, and there is nothing more futile than trying to get two toddlers to sleep in the same room. They are worse than a frat house. They are totally down to party all night, scream and yell, and hype each other up if one of them shows any signs of im-pending sleep. I had to stagger nap schedules so each kid could have a private room to nap and not be woken up by a sibling, which meant I never got a moment alone during naps like I did with one kid. I had a pack-and-play in just about every corner of the house, so anyplace could serve as a quiet corner where a kid could sleep.

In an ideal world, my day would include a shower and makeup application, three healthy meals, a good walk/run, time to check email/Facebook, time to read, a quality conversation with a friend, a clean house, a couple cycles of laundry completed, and a few errands run. Surprisingly, none of these things were on the priority list for my kids.

But there were some beautiful lessons in having all of my kids close in age, namely, that I absolutely *had* to let myself off the hook. You can try to do things perfectly with one kid. You can even chase the illusion with two. But with four? You *know* you are outnumbered. Not only can you not do it all perfectly, but you don't even have the energy to try. Pretty quickly I learned to take myself less seriously.

Intentionally or not, you parent third and fourth kids differently. It's no longer about all the newest toys and cutest clothes. It's no longer about making sure each child has had the right amount of visual stimulation. It's no longer about making sure a child is always happy and involved in activities that will, "according to research," make them the smartest kid in the class.

It's about survival. For you *and* for them.

Moms of multiple kids go with the flow. We make sacrifices and lower some standards in order to give our attention to more important things. We do things we never would have done as a first-time parent, things that weren't even on our radar when we changed that very first diaper. Things we don't always even admit to in mixed company.

Here are a few other examples of how we change with the brave souls who join our families last.

1. We pick a pacifier up off the floor and pop it right back in a kid's mouth. Without washing it. Or we wash it with our own motherly saliva, which is virtually as pure and clean as sanitizing gel, I've been told.*

2. At age eight, our first child is allowed one educational program a day. At age eight, the last child is on season three of *Dexter*. Our first child wasn't allowed videogames. Our last child runs their own Fortnite-playing YouTube channel.

3. We pretty much give up on all the baby-proofing products because we know that much sooner than we expect, they are going to learn to crawl out of that crib/undo the straps of that high chair/scale the top of that baby gate/undo the catch on the kitchen cabinet.

4. Our first child is required to try to eat every vegetable on their plate. Our last child eats only products made of white flour or cheese. We give them "food" products we would never eat. Dinosaur-shaped frozen chicken nuggets. Flat, sticky, um . . . fruit . . . that arrives rolled in plastic. Crackers with peanut-butter-flavored filling.

5. We believe in the five-second rule: It's *science*. We pick up dropped snacks off the floor at home and let our children eat them. Really, if I sit my kid in the high chair to eat but over half the food gets on the floor, and then they want to crawl around on the floor and eat the food, wouldn't it be more efficient to just put the food on the floor to begin with? (I will remain silent on whether or not I tried this.)

6. When our first kid was injured we took a trip to urgent care. Our last kid is not going to the doctor for any unplanned

---

* No one has told me this.

reason unless there is a fear of imminent death. It's ambulance-level trauma or we are staying home. *You probably didn't need that little tip of your thumb you just cut off, anyway. Grab a Band-Aid and try not to get blood everywhere.*

7. With our first kid: *I will meet all his needs, I am his mama, it's my job!*

   With our last kid: *Here.* TAKE HER.

8. When our first child tries to jump off the roof into the pool, we put them in time-out. When our last child does it, we grab our camera.

9. We keep all the leftovers. Anyone's leftovers. We go to dinner with friends and they leave some food on their plates? I'll take it to go and feed it to a kid tomorrow.

10. We leave them home alone far earlier than we did with the older kids, who had a babysitter until they were thirteen. The youngest is left home alone at seven with a cellphone and instructions to text if anything weird happens.

11. Our older kids enter preschool already knowing their shapes, colors, letters, and numbers. Our youngest kid enters pre-school knowing some curse words and how to hit back.

12. When our first baby cries, we hop out of the shower, wet and with shampoo in our hair, to attend to them. When our second baby cries, we stay in the shower. When our third baby cries, maybe it's time to take a shower?

13. With our first child, we spend thirty minutes reading them their books of choice every night, maybe even with voices. With our last child, we pick out one or two sentences to read per page, trying to skip pages without them noticing, and

hide the super-long, boring books that we just don't feel like reading. (I'm looking at you, *Blueberries for Sal* and just about every Dr. Seuss book ever.)

14. Our first child licks dirt off his hands and we call poison control. Our last child eats a handful of leaves and we praise them for their flexible palate.

15. With our first kid, when the teacher sends home a form at the beginning of the year asking us to tell them about our child, we write a thoughtful two-page essay detailing their psycho-social development, their strengths and weaknesses, the special quirks of their personality, their insecurities, and their hopes and dreams. With our last kid we scribble a distracted paragraph that sounds more like a rushed Yelp review. *Typical kid. 7/10. Would have again.*

It's interesting, though. The mother of four that I've become is probably healthier than the mom I was with my first two. I started as a tightly wound bundle of nerves who worried I was harming my baby for life because he wouldn't eat green beans. Now I'm a mom who watches four kids have a food fight on the front porch, laughing, because they'll remember this for the rest of their lives.

SKIN IN THE GAME

When we identify where our privilege intersects with somebody else's oppression, we'll find our opportunities to make real change.

IJEOMA OLUO

On paper, two of my kids appear to be twins. They share the same last name and the same date of birth. However, one was born in Laguna Beach, California, and one was born in Mirebalais, Haiti. One has blond hair, blue eyes, and pale skin; the other has dark brown skin, brown eyes, and black hair. The shared birthday was unintentional, a weird and curious coincidence to have been matched for adoption with a child born on the same day as my biological child. We've jokingly referred to them as "the twins" ever since.

It has led to some funny moments, especially in new schools when the teacher, based on the roster, expects to see twins that look more alike than they do.

I will also admit to having used the assumptions around their birthdays to my advantage. There is a good magnet school near our house. But they get more applicants than they have spots every year so students are selected via a lottery. One of my twins got in, and one didn't. The school called me and explained that they would make an exception for twins. "I mean, they shared a womb!" the administrator said. "We can't separate them." It is possible I did not correct her on the technicalities of their births. And it's possible we showed up to school on the first day and caused a lot of confusion.

Their twin status has also allowed me to observe the way the world treats them differently. I have two kids of the exact same age, but frequently India is viewed as younger and Kembe is seen as older. This is consistent with a plethora of research studies showing that black children are judged older or more dangerous beginning as young as five. My black boys are more likely to be questioned about what they are doing and to be treated with suspicion at times when my white girls are given a pass. For example, we were at a restaurant and my daughter went and asked for a cup of water and was given one. My son went up to the same counter and was told he needed to be a "paying customer." (Which he was.)

My boys have been asked if they belong somewhere much more often than their white sisters, but I also observe disparities with how their white friends are treated. My oldest son was threatened with arrest for cutting through a college campus on his skateboard at age twelve, while none of his other (white) skating friends have ever been threatened with arrest. Microaggressions like this happen all the time, and it places an unfair burden on my boys, who just want to be kids.

The tragedies of Trayvon Martin, Tamir Rice, Eric Garner, and Philando Castile, and the disproportionate number of unarmed black men shot by police, illustrate the importance of teaching my boys that they will have to navigate the world differently as black men. This is what I know to be true about raising black boys: It's imperative for me to teach them that based on their skin color some people will look at them with suspicion or stereotype. I don't share that experience, and so I have to enlist other people to help guide them through this reality. It's also important that they feel a sense of pride in their own race. That's why it's important that black adopted children in white families have strong black role models in their lives. We've worked hard to make sure that has been available to them, and I'm incredibly grateful for the black mentors who have helped shape their racial identity. I want to give my kids agency in owning and telling their own unique experience as transracial adoptees. I'm admittedly focused on sharing my own experience as an adoptive parent as opposed to trying to translate the perspectives of two young men growing up in a white family. But I will say that as teenagers, both of my kids express a great deal of pride in being black, and Kembe feels very proud to be Haitian.

Learning how to infuse my black sons with a healthy racial identity has been a serious lesson in humility. The first step was confronting my own racial privilege. I initially heard the phrase "white privilege" in my twenties. I didn't like it. How could I be privileged? I paid for my own college. I paid for my own car. I was broke. Shitty things happened to me. I didn't feel privileged by any stretch. I thought white privilege dismissed the very real hardships and challenges that I've had in my life. I thought white privilege meant that I had to apologize for things that happened before I was born, or that I needed to be ashamed or embarrassed for being born white.

I realize now that white privilege isn't about me individually. It's not a personal attack. White privilege is a systemic cultural reality that I can either choose to ignore, or choose to acknowledge and attempt to change. It has nothing to do with my worth as a person or my own personal struggle. "Privilege" refers to an unearned advantage. It usually refers to something inherent, something you were born with rather than something you worked for. There are many types of privilege: economic privilege, gender privilege, heterosexual privilege, able-bodied privilege, and of course, racial privilege. It was important for me to learn the difference between these types of privilege.

For example, my protest that "I had a black friend who was raised with way more money than me so how can I be the privileged one?" was me confusing racial privilege with socioeconomic privilege. One kind of privilege doesn't negate an unrelated kind of privilege. We're not playing Oppression Olympics. When we ignore one form of privilege because another exists, we're being dismissive. The fact that I'm white does not mean that I don't sometimes experience sexism. The fact that a black person was born to a wealthy family doesn't mean they never experience racism. In that instance, when I denied white privilege existed because there are other forms of privilege, I was refusing to look at the racial biases other people face every day regardless of their financial situations.

At its essence, it's a simple concept: White privilege refers to the both minor and significant advantages that white people hold in American society. Racial privilege can take minor forms and it can take life-threatening forms. Racial privilege is both unearned and is always at the expense of people of color. A minor version of white privilege is walking into a grocery store and being confident they carry shampoo for your hair type, or being able to find a Band-Aid that matches your skin tone. More seriously, white privilege may allow you to walk through an upscale residential neighborhood without anyone wondering what you are doing there. It may allow you to wear a baseball cap and baggy pants without people assuming you are a criminal. It may allow you to get argumentative with a cop without fear of being shot.

A few years ago, I woke up to the sound of glass breaking. I did what I'd been trained to do if I thought there might be a break-in: I immediately called the police. They responded and came to the door, and asked to search our house and yard. The kids were still sleeping. As they searched the backyard, with guns held up in front of their chests asking an intruder to make himself known, they woke Jafta and he screamed and ran down the hall into my room. And I had the thought. What if at that moment the cops had been in the house, with their guns in hand, and saw a black male, who is as tall as many adults but only twelve years old, come barreling down the hallway? What might have happened as they searched for an intruder when they saw a panicked black male who didn't fit what they might expect a family member of mine to look like?

Everything ended well. We discovered the noise was an animal breaking a planter in the neighbor's yard and Jafta ended up safely tucked back in his bed. But it was hard going back to sleep with the vision of what could have happened. I couldn't help but think of Tamir Rice, who was the same size as my sons and was gunned down in broad daylight while playing with a toy in the park.

In retrospect, I should have identified all members of our household, and their race, to the 911 dispatcher and again to the police before letting them in. Not because I think all police officers are racists, but because we are all swimming in this insidious bias that can be life-threatening, and that requires careful attention. It was a reminder to me that black people have to be constantly vigilant in every interaction with law enforcement. It was also a reminder that white people need to be careful if and when they decide to involve police in a situation with people of color. Because of my white privilege I called without immediately considering the consequences.

There is nothing threatening about acknowledging privilege. Being more empathetic to the experiences of others is not a sacrifice of personal politics or lifestyle. Feelings of guilt about white privilege should occur only if, because you don't experience racism, you decide you don't have to listen or care when other people do, or because you refuse to give up privileges that you keep at the expense of others.

White people have a hard time recognizing our own culture. We are swimming in it, so we assume that white culture is just "normal" or default. Even the word "ethnic" refers to someone being non-white, as if white is the absence of ethnicity. When we don't acknowledge that some of our cultural norms or traditions are uniquely white, rather than universally human, we resent when others deviate from our traditions or celebrate their own. This is the reason people get perturbed when there is a Mexican fiesta at their child's school. It's the reason people whine about Black History Month. It's the reason we ask a question like When is it gonna be OUR day? (If you live in America, it's EVERY DAY.)

I have a theory. I think that if white people start to understand what it means to be white, that they would begin to relate more to people of color with less defensiveness. Acknowledging whiteness helps white people understand that they, too, are having a race-based experience. If we identify our own cultural norms and traditions, we don't need to feel threatened by celebrating the culture of another. If we understand the negative aspects of our culture and we commit to making changes, then we don't have to feel defensive about owning the history of oppression that is also inherent in white privilege. We can acknowledge our affinity for Jon Stewart and Gap and Cracker Barrel and NASCAR and Whole Foods, while at the same time having enough humility to be mindful of the ways our white privilege might come into play.

Like when we write this chapter using the first-person plural, creating the narrative that my readers are also white and not considering how this might alienate and annoy any non-white readers.

Yep. White privilege. I'm still working on it.

VWAZINAJ SE FANMI
(THE NEIGHBORHOOD IS THE FAMILY)

The beggarly question of parentage—what is it, after all? What does it matter, when you come to think of it, whether a child is yours by blood or not? All the little ones of our time are collectively the children of us adults of the time, and entitled to our general care.

THOMAS HARDY

When I was growing up, there were always extra kids around our house. My dad worked at a college, and we would often have students stay with us over the weekends or even over summers when they couldn't afford to get home. One of my friends in high school had some trouble at home and she moved in with us and slept on the trundle that pulled out from below my brass daybed for the better part of a year. My youngest sister had a friend over for a sleepover and while with us, her mother took her own life. She never left.

My mom was notorious for packing as many kids as she could into her minivan. This was before the strict seat belt laws and we would sit two-to-a-seat, and then wedge people into the trunk and even into the doorwell. Before youth group on Wednesday nights she would drive across town picking up anyone who wanted to join us, and then she would drive everyone home. It probably added an hour to the evening, and I can't even imagine how loud we all were, laughing as we were squished together in that van.

My home was chaotic. There was a lot of yelling. We were late everywhere. Our second language was Passive-Aggressive, and we were also familiar with Christianese Shame. But my mom never met a kid she didn't like, at least a little bit. My family was a mess, but kids felt welcome there. And as a result, you never knew how many places to set at the dinner table until it was time to eat. Having someone over, having a friend stay for dinner, having a friend spend the night. The answer was always yes.

I've worked hard to be a home that kids want to come to. This might sound like a humble-brag but in reality there is some selfish motivation behind it: When they have friends over, my kids are less bored and therefore bother me less. At any given time we have an extra kid or three in the house. We've got a pool and a skate ramp, because I'd rather have kids here under my eye than getting into trouble somewhere else. The result is that my house is often an explosion of children. There are kids skating in the driveway and sitting on top of the playhouse we converted into a little library that is now a "hangout spot." The neighbors with grown children look at us and laugh. The parents with very small children look on in horror. One exasperated neighbor of two toddlers once said to me, "There are just too many children here all the time. It isn't safe." And I remember thinking that I was gonna have to try super hard not to be smug when his kids become teenagers.

We currently have two foreign exchange students from Myanmar living with us for the semester. Last semester, it was a college student from India. The year prior, right before we went on our own trip to Tokyo, we hosted four students from Japan. It isn't always easy. Sometimes the language and cultural barriers are downright awkward.

On our first morning hosting Japanese students, I had set out a tea spread for them, not really paying attention to which teas I pulled out from the cabinet. I later came back to find every last one of them had picked a laxative tea that produces explosive diarrhea in about three hours. I only discovered this by finding four empty mugs of Smooth Move tea next to the sink. This left me with a sticky ethical dilemma. Do I explain this to them using some kind of miming? Do I Google Translate it and read, "You are going to have explosive diarrhea soon" in broken Japanese? Or do I just let nature run its course? I chose the latter, the other options seemed too mortifying.

There have been other cross-cultural foibles. On the first day the Burmese students stayed with us, they decided to walk to Target *and brought the shopping cart home with them.* But despite the occasional moments of awkwardness, my kids benefit from interacting with teenagers from other parts of the world, and they learn that some things we assume are just normal teen behaviors are decidedly *American* teen behaviors. The visitors we have hosted have displayed none of the angst and attitude and eye-rolling inherent in the American teenage existence. They have been respectful, deferential, and lovely. They mostly just made me annoyed at my own kids. The Japanese students would stand at their seats and wait to sit down until I was seated. Meanwhile my own children were already eating. Their entire stay was mostly consumed with me pointing out the respect the

Japanese teens showed and giving dirty looks to my American barbarians.

On my little street there are a handful of moms who treat my kids like their own. They will feed them, but also discipline them when necessary. They are ready with a Band-Aid and also a lecture on head injuries and wearing your helmet. These are moms who know my kids' personality quirks well enough to recognize when someone needs to be pulled out of a game, or when one of them is lying. They are also moms that I can call in a crisis. Without a question they would house and feed my kids for the night, or for the week. There is a Haitian proverb, *Vwazinaj se fanmi,* that translates to "the neighborhood is the family." I am grateful to be a part of this community approach to child-rearing.

I actually like it when other people discipline my kids. I feel like it provides an outside push to be better. Often, they will take adult input more seriously when they hear it from someone else. I may have asked them to stop kicking the seat in front of them on the plane three times, but when the passenger ahead of them asks them to stop, *it just got serious.* If my kids are being assholes, I absolutely invite other adults to step in and offer a correction. When another adult corrects my child I usually raise an eyebrow and give a look to my child that says, *See? Not just me.*

I have also been the mom at the park telling another kid to stop hitting. Just the other day, I drove past two middle-school boys punching the crap out of each other and I did a U-turn, pulled up alongside, and told them in the scariest mom voice I could muster to let go of each other. My middle-schooler literally ducked down in the front seat out of mortification. *Don't care*. If your kid is being a jerk to someone else, I will let them know.

Our kids are not special snowflakes who can only handle input from Mom or Dad. They will live in a world where they will have to deal with authority, from teachers to bosses. I want my kids to learn to accept feedback from other people. But more than anything, I want my kids to understand that their behaviors affect other people. If their running into an elevator almost knocks someone over, if their loud talking at a restaurant is annoying to others, if their coughing without putting a hand up to their mouth puts someone at risk of germs, I'm totally okay with my kids hearing that from the person they are bothering. In fact, I'm especially okay with them hearing it from people they are bothering, so they can learn to have more empathy.

I really do think that it takes a village, and when we shelter our kids from feedback from other adults, I think it gives them a sense of entitlement. Sometimes it can be a hit to the pride when our kids need to be corrected by strangers, but if we can monitor our defensiveness, our kids will benefit from being in a community where other adults are helping to guide them, as well.

To me, taking a posture of concern for other people's kids is also just *the right thing to do*. I think this is what drew me to adoption. Even as a teenager, I was bothered by the notion that children were growing up without families. I wanted to provide a home for children who didn't have one. Perhaps the biggest full-circle moment of this notion of universal parenting came when we reunited with Jafta's birthfather. We had lost contact with him after Jafta's adoption. There are circumstances in which social services orders a closed adoption, and that was the case for Jafta. Like so many parents who lose custody of their children, Jafta's father had grown up in the system himself. As a young father, he was still struggling with the trauma of his childhood, which led to addiction and, ultimately, incarceration.

When Jafta was twelve years old, his birthfather found me and reached out. He wanted to develop a relationship. They exchanged photos and letters and we began planning a visit when, suddenly and unexpectedly, he passed away. Jafta and I went to his funeral, where we got to hear his friends and family stand up and speak of what he meant to them. Over and over, we heard people talk of how he was a "father to many." He had lost custody of his biological children, but went on to turn his life around and become a doting stepfather to two girls. He was a popular "cheer dad" and volunteer in their activities, where he was regarded as a kind and gentle father figure. As I sat there listening to these stories, I was struck with emotion. As I was raising his son that he had not been ready to care for, he had later gone on to parent children who were not his biologically. Family extends beyond blood in so many directions. It was devastating to both of us that we never got to meet him, but I am so grateful that Jafta got to hear such a loving account of this man. His widow and I still stay in touch, forming a new kind of extended family in his memory.

I would argue that it is the best of our humanity when we see every human being as worthy of love, and every child as deserving as our own. This type of "global parenting" is not practiced exclusively by mothers. It's done by volunteers who advocate for foster kids in court, it's done by people who offer childcare to struggling families in their community, it's done by activists who write letters and make phone calls to make sure kids are not separated from their parents at the border. It was done by the seventy-year-old foster mom who cared for Jafta for months before a family was found for him. It was done by the loving nannies in Haiti who cared for Kembe for three years. It can be grand gestures, or it can be a simple kindness. Or it can be telling a kid throwing sand at other kids that he needs to chill or you'll find his parent.

DOES THIS DIVORCE MAKE MY BRAND LOOK BAD?

When we are no longer able to change a situation, we are challenged to change ourselves.

VIKTOR FRANKL

I t's hard to explain why I was so keen to get married quickly out of high school, to a pastor, no less, unless you've grown up in the particular brand of conservative Christianity I was raised in. Christianity was not about a relationship with the God of the universe. It was not about modeling your life after Jesus through service to the poor or advocacy for the oppressed. It was about *rules*. It was a club with members who didn't do a specific list of things. Namely, drinking, smoking, cussing, drugs, and sex.

By the time I left high school, despite my earlier promises to myself and the group around the campfire at church camp, I had engaged in all of those behaviors. I was a classic pastor's daughter stereotype. I showed up to church every Sunday, but I was a party girl on Friday and Saturday night. After a childhood in which I was pushed to perform, to pretend, and to appear perfect, with a bit of religious guilt sprinkled on top for good measure, I fractured under the weight of the rules.

At church, we were taught that we were undeserving sinners who were saved by the grace of God. The emphasis was always on the undeserving part and I felt that keenly. I took communion every Sunday and thought of the things I had done wrong that week, internally flagellating myself for being such a piece of shit. Rather than seeing communion as a time to meditate in the presence of a loving God, I saw it as a time to beat myself up over how unworthy I was. I spent most of my teen years living in a state of turmoil about my faith, and wallowing in guilt and shame.

I went to college a two-days' drive from my hometown, anxious to forge a new path. And, of course, to meet a husband. I was still ignited by religious zeal and archaic views of a woman's role, so I went to Bible college in order to nail down a Good Christian Boy. I wanted to be married, preferably to someone whose outward expression of faith would relieve some of my inner shame for past transgressions.

The college I attended was tied to the denomination I was raised in, in which my father was ordained. Students were not allowed to wear shorts, to dance, to have piercings, or even to play cards. We had to sign a behavior contract that said that not only would we refrain from drinking, smoking, and fornication, but that we would rat out any classmates who indulged.

As a party girl from Florida accustomed to spending her weekends drinking and dancing at the club, I was totally out of place at a conservative midwestern Bible college. But instead of perceiving it as the wrong fit, or maybe even an indictment of the college's culture, I blamed myself. I was wayward. I was messed up. Broken. I was convinced that I needed to fit in to prove my worth to God. And when you are an immature, shame-ridden teenager who thinks that outward appearances are the way to God's heart, what better way to sanctify yourself than by marrying a pastor? So that's what I set out to do.

I met a boy my first day on campus. He was funny and charismatic. He was a surfer from California, and was a darling at the college. He was one of the school's student ambassadors and often spoke at chapel. He was on a path to be a youth pastor. And it didn't hurt that he was tall and cute. Unlike me, he'd spent his teen years leading a Bible study that resulted in evangelizing a good portion of his school. He was, as they say, *on fire for God*. I could picture a life with him. One where I was proud of my husband, serving alongside him as a dutiful "smoking hot wife." (If you are not entrenched in Christian culture, this is how just about every pastor refers to his wife from the pulpit. Because objectification is okay *if you are married*.)

Soon after, we were dating. A year later, engaged. We were married during my junior year of college. I was barely legal to drink, had never lived on my own, and yet made the biggest decision of my life because I was just so grateful that I had found a good Christian guy who was willing to marry me despite my being a "used piece of chewing gum," as one youth pastor crassly described those girls who gave their bodies away before marriage. Marrying a pastor: Achievement unlocked.

My new husband and I moved to California, where I attended grad school and worked my ass off to finish my psychotherapy internship in record time. By twenty-four, I was a licensed therapist working in private practice, checking steps off my perfect plan along the way. My husband was working as a youth pastor. I'd work a little longer, we'd buy a house, and then we'd have some kids. I assumed life would follow that road map.

Except that it didn't. Three years into our marriage, my husband had something to tell me. And there in our little house, in the living room I had so carefully curated, he told me things that broke apart the picture I had of my perfect Christian husband. The details are his to tell, but the betrayal is my own story to share. I was twenty-four, and scared. I had moved to the other side of the country for grad school and my only friends were the people I'd met through the church my husband was working with. I was embarrassed and ashamed, and while his proclivities would be a nonissue in a regular job, I knew that telling anyone in our church circle would likely mean he'd lose his ministry job. We were broke and living in one of the most expensive counties in the country. I felt lucky to have found a guy who would take me "damaged." But who would take me divorced? I wondered. I had no concept of my own self-worth.

I told no one. I read misguided Christian books on forgiveness that reminded me that a good Christian girl makes her marriage work, no matter what. We went to twelve-step groups and marriage conferences on keeping promises, and he vowed to change. I told myself that I was forgiving him in the same way he'd forgiven me for things I'd done before I'd even met him. Here I was, with the man who was supposed to redeem my failings, learning in the hardest way I could imagine that my feelings of worthlessness were mine alone to heal.

I struggled with blaming myself. I knew that he was in the wrong, but I also began to scheme how I could prevent future missteps. Maybe if I worked out more. Maybe if I got a boob job. Maybe if I was prettier/sexier/easier. The burden of so many wives married to men with a roving eye is wondering what flaws we could fix to mitigate the problem. As if the problem was ours to fix. Unfortunately, church culture only reinforced this. "If the barn needs painting, ladies," we are told. Keep your husband interested, not with witty banter or emotional connection, but by putting on lipstick and maybe some lingerie. Purity culture said that if another guy was giving too much attention to your body, it was your fault for "making him stumble." But it also subtly implied that keeping your husband's wandering attention solely focused on you was your responsibility, too.

I wish I could go back and tell that girl that forgiveness does not mean staying in a bad relationship. That you can forgive someone and also distance yourself. That divorced does not mean broken. That hiding a husband's issues from your only friends and living in isolated turmoil is no way to live. That the feedback of friends speaking into your private pain is invaluable and empowering and necessary. But it took me twenty years to get to a point where I could share the issues that plagued my marriage with other people.

The problem is that when you don't share your real life with others, others don't really know you, so you always feel alone. Intimacy with friends isn't based on sharing every last detail of your life. But it does require a willingness to admit to your closest friends that things are harder than they appear. If you want to avoid being painfully isolated, you have to be willing to share what's causing you the greatest grief.

I was skilled at hiding my negative feelings. I presented a stoic exterior because I feared spilling my feelings on anyone else, like they were a stain. This fear was present in my childhood and was reinforced in my marriage. A therapist once told me I was like a duck, gliding peacefully on top of the water but paddling desperately and clumsily underneath. "Being a duck" became a metaphor for me trying to present a false sense of serenity and perfection to the world. When it came to my marriage, I was often being a duck.

Those twenty years were not all bad. When we worked, we worked well. My husband was a spontaneous and enthusiastic extrovert. He loved adventure and travel. I longed to be more adventurous, but I brought a stabilizing force to his wild ideas. He was the dreamer, I was the implementer. (If you know the Enneagram, he was a 7, always looking for a good time, and I was a 3, always wanting to perform and be productive.) He encouraged me to take life less seriously, to get out of my comfort zone, and to take risks. I made his zeal for adventure a reality. He broadened our social circle with his outgoing charisma; I deepened and maintained our friendships by making plans. We traveled a ton, we threw lots of parties, and we had loads of fun.

We were a great team in our twenties and thirties as a childless, two-income couple. But when life got hard, the cracks began to show. I found him to be entitled, irresponsible, and lazy. He found me to be controlling, stifling, and a workaholic. I felt that if he would step it up, I wouldn't have to work so hard and could finally relax for a minute. He felt I should just relax anyway. These personality differences are not marriage-ending. But they led to resentments and bitterness that fueled the ongoing issues that did end the marriage.

My husband barely resembled the passionate pastor I had married. When we left the scaffolding of the church and the inherent moral rules of a pastor's life, my husband leaned in a very different direction. He went out a lot. I spent many evenings at home alone. I started to feel like a babysitter rather than a wife. We barely spoke beyond the perfunctory issues of co-parenting and running a house together.

Amid the overwhelm of having four kids, the disparities in

the effort that my husband and I contributed to keeping our marriage afloat became even more apparent. If I didn't schedule a counseling appointment, it didn't happen. If I didn't schedule a date night, it didn't happen. I could count on one hand the number of times my husband planned and implemented a date night in our twenty years together. It started to feel like I was the one carrying *everything* . . . the house, the kids, the marriage. "I feel like a housekeeper that you sleep with," I told him often. I was exhausted and burnt out. He was not. I remember hearing someone say to me once, "He who cares less, holds all the control." That could not have been more true in my marriage. I was distraught about the state of our relationship, but my husband did not seem to care. At one point, I tried to talk to him about how bad things were. "I cry myself to sleep just about every night," I told him. His response: "I'm not shedding any tears about this." And he wasn't. He was content with the way things were. I was holding down the fort at home. He was living what he (actually, out loud) referred to as a European Lifestyle, which by his definition meant he worked about twenty hours a week and enjoyed going out several nights a week. I'm guessing this point is fairly obvious, but with four kids, I was not, in fact, also living my own European Lifestyle.

I started seeing a therapist by myself. She encouraged me that it was time to let go of managing everything by myself. *Give him a chance to step up, or at least feel what happens when you don't. You can only change yourself.* So I did.

I got off the hamster wheel that I was running on, alone, to keep my marriage going. What if I don't plan the dates? What if I relax on the constant dieting to keep my body at a weight that felt impossible to maintain but required to be attractive? What if I start confronting the inequities instead of avoiding them?

What if my feelings are spoken instead of stuffed? What if I'm less winsome and more honest? What if I don't participate in the physical requests of intimacy if there is no reciprocation in the other aspects of the relationship?

When I stopped trying to keep the wheels on my marriage, they pretty much fell off. We started sleeping in separate bedrooms. I woke up on my twentieth wedding anniversary in my bed alone. I wondered if we would acknowledge this usually celebrated milestone of two decades together. I didn't say anything to him and he avoided me all day. At some point, he quietly went to bed in his own room, and I burst into tears.

I found myself in the same spot I did when I was twenty-four, in a messed-up relationship with habits that I was not comfortable with. But this time, I was a little older and a little wiser. And this time, I had a circle of friends I knew I could trust with anything, and I sought their counsel. I was no longer afraid to talk about the reality of my marriage with people I trusted. And deep down, I knew I should leave.

I was worried about the impact this would have on my kids. They were all still in elementary school. I knew the statistics on divorce. I'd been a therapist. I knew it was a trauma. But I also had to consider what I was modeling for my kids. We tend to marry into systems that are similar to what we grew up with. I know I did. I did not want that for my kids. I did not want them to think that this strained and unbalanced relationship was normal.

Several days before Christmas in the twenty-first year of our marriage, I filed for divorce. But our marriage had already been over long before that day.

The hardest moment of the end of my marriage was telling my kids about it. We did everything we could to soften it. We were going to continue living in the same house (and did for a while). We would still do holidays together. *We would always be a family. Nothing was their fault.* We said all of the things that we hoped would make it easier, but still. They were devastated. I felt immense grief for the pain this caused them, and still causes them.

I desperately wanted to stay married. I did not want to be a single mom. I got married and wanted to be married to that person for life. I believe in marriage, so much so that I dedicated my graduate studies and the first decade of my professional life to helping people have healthy marriages. And yet, as a marriage counselor, I could not save my own. I felt deep shame about that. Staying married was the greatest goal of my life, and I was crushed when my marriage failed.

I had been incredibly private about my marital issues, due to paralyzing fears of what people would think. I became skilled at playing the part of a happy couple and glossing over things going on at home. I wanted to believe my marriage was as good as I could make it look in a photo or a Christmas card. I let myself believe that optics could control outcomes. I let myself believe that the narrative I told was a true one. Getting a divorce meant having to relinquish the illusion, and that was really hard for me. And in the midst of wanting desperately to hide, I had to continue as a public person online because that's how I support myself. Navigating a public life through private pain was demoralizing and exhausting.

The first few years post-divorce were some of the darkest of my life. Many days, not crying in public or in front of my kids was the best I could do. I would lie in bed at night, alone in a house with four kids, and feel like I was in a free fall. It felt like the world was crumbling under my feet. The nights without the kids were worse. Being in an empty house felt unbearable. It was a struggle not to cry each time they packed their backpacks to go to Dad's house. Walking by their empty rooms at night took my breath away.

For most women who divorce, it is also financially devastating. In addition to the emotional fallout, I was also dealing with instability and insecurity about how I would afford to live on my own. I was in massive debt. I was having panic attacks about losing my house, and what that additional loss would feel like to the kids. I was working sixty-plus hours a week to make ends meet. I didn't feel like I had any time for self-care. I wondered, regularly, if I should have just stayed married because my new life felt so hard. But I knew that I was ultimately doing the right thing, no matter how painful it was in the transition.

I had to stay off social media because seeing photos of happy couples was triggering. Anniversary tributes put me into a spiral. Every holiday, as happy family photos popped up, I felt the grief of knowing that my photo looked different than I ever thought it would.

I had to reframe the narrative about my life. I had to remove "be married for life" as a goalpost for having a successful life. I had to transform my idea of family and believe that my kids and I were still a whole and valid family even if I was single. I had to see myself as worthy, alone, of all the things I felt worthy of as a part of a couple. I took family portraits with just myself and the kids, even though at first it felt foreign and pathetic. I took my kids on family vacations myself, even though at first it felt sad and lonely being the only adult. I cooked good, healthy meals even if most of the kids complained about them, because I was worth making a meal from scratch even if there was not another adult at the table. I had to go through the motions of doing those things until they felt natural and until doing things alone became my new normal. Now, when I take my kids on trips, I enjoy their company and bring books and movies to enjoy by myself after they go to bed. I push hard at the subliminal messages I've swallowed that say that doing any of these things without a spouse somehow lessens the experience.

I grieved the twenty-one-year-old girl who was so relieved to be married, and had such high expectations. I grieved the idea of a long-standing marriage. I very much grieved not being married to the father of my children, and how that severing created stress and anxiety in their lives. I grieved for my kids, and the pain of not living with both of their parents full-time.

We were able to have a very private divorce even though I am a somewhat public person, but I did finally feel the need to address my divorce publicly. I didn't want to, and there were many times that I just wanted to crawl into a hole of anonymity. I thought about just closing up shop and walking away from the blog and the world of "Internet platforms" because I felt so exposed. In order to live truthfully I had to walk into a firestorm of potential judgment: a public Christian, getting a divorce, with rumors swirling on- and off-line. I've been seeking approval from others my whole life. Admitting my divorce publicly meant I needed to push the approval-seeking aside, and it was terrifying and anxiety-provoking. But it was also empowering. It was an amazing feeling to shut out the opinion of "everyone" and focus on the counsel of my inner circle and the care of my kids. It was like I put on a pair of blinders that focused me in on the people who actually mattered.

Thankfully, once I went public with my divorce, I found that people were much less judgmental than I had imagined they would be. Sure, there were some doozies. The friend who told me, "If you leave him, you'll just end up with a guy with a different set of problems." The mom from school who reminded me, "Marriage is about waking up and forgiving every day." There are people who think I've taken the easy way out. (News flash: Being a primary-custody single mom to four kids is *not* the easy way out.) But overwhelmingly, people approached me with great empathy. People came out of the woodwork to reach out and share their own marriage struggles, their personal divorce stories, or their personal fears and ambivalence around divorce. This has been true every single time I've opened up about painful experiences. My instinct is to keep the mask up, but every time I push to vulnerability, I find that I am immediately enveloped by others who have walked the same path. You would think that I would have learned to stop trying to pretend sooner, but some lessons are hard-won, and some habits are deeply ingrained.

At first, I had to pretend that I would put on a brave face to shake off the criticisms and passive-aggressive comments that let me know people were disappointed in me. But after a while, it mattered less. My girlfriends and I would laugh at each new slight. Eventually, I really stopped caring what random acquaintances or strangers thought of me. I'm now putting that accomplishment right into the "life-goal achieved" slot where "stay married until I die" used to sit. It's more realistic, it's within my own control, and it will serve me well in every scenario I find myself in.

Divorce is one of the hardest things I've been through. I can't say I'm following my truth or that we're all better off. It's shitty. For everyone. We're doing the best we can, but it's still hard. Being the single parent of four active kids is mind-numbingly exhausting. But the beauty of the past few years is that I've had to face the demons of people-pleasing, and slay them. I weathered the storm and came out the other side, and found clarity and inner strength that I didn't possess at the beginning of the journey.

Now, when I look at our family portraits, I don't see a sad single mom. I see a happy, complete family.

TYPE-A MOM, B+ FAMILY: EXCELLING AT AVERAGE

There is no way to be a perfect mother,
and a million ways to be a good one.

JILL CHURCHILL

When I was a kid, my favorite toy was a battery. Except in our elaborate fantasy world of James Bond, it wasn't a battery. *It was a bomb.* My best friend, Crystal, and I would gather our friends, and give everyone appropriate "Bond Girl" names like Vesper or Tatiana. Then we would plot our mission, our alter-personalities, and our Bond Girl outfits and hairdos. Eventually we would wrangle Crystal's older brother into being James Bond, which involved him throwing a battery at us as we counted and ran away from the explosion.

My second favorite thing to do was to make up dance routines to Madonna's *True Blue* album. Or to ride my bike around my neighborhood and see who else was outside that might want to ride bikes with me. While I'm sure I had moments of feeling bored, that is not the dominant memory of my childhood. My memories involve exploring and pretending and daydreaming.

With today's intense pressure to get your kids involved in every possible activity, there have been seasons when every minute of my kids' lives have been scheduled. As a result, they haven't always experienced the beauty of boredom that leads to unstructured, creative play. That type of free play is essential to the physical, social, and emotional well-being of kids. It helps them to discover their interests and abilities, to handle problems on their own, and to manage their time. It lets kids be kids for a while.

When I'm not micromanaging or overscheduling them, I see my four active, opinionated, and vocal children cooperate and find solutions to the conflicts that inevitably arise. Without me, they have unstructured fun together in creative ways, learning to negotiate without my input. When they were younger they created a cupcake store, or made a Lego world. Now that they are older they practice skateboard tricks or write plays or play board games with their own rules.

I don't remember my own mom being a present, hot-glue-gun-supervising chaperone at every holiday elementary school party of my childhood. Hell, I don't even remember elementary school holiday celebrations. I mean, I'm sure we had them, but they were not the every-parent-present productions that they are today. I think my mom came to my classroom twice a year. Meanwhile, I feel guilty if I don't attend every class party, even for fake holidays that shouldn't be an event. (Pi Day and Dr. Seuss Day and 100 Days of School, I'm looking at you.) There are so many celebrations and so many trophies. And so many opportunities to celebrate mediocrity. And so many expectations to meet.

When Jafta was eight years old, he walked into the living room the night before St. Patrick's Day, and asked, "Can I help you guys hide the gold coins?"

The *what*?

"The gold coins. I know the leprechauns aren't real," he said, wise older brother. "I know it's you, like Santa. So I want to help you. I can make the leprechaun trap, too."

We told Jafta to go to bed. Then we looked at each other with exasperation. Gold coins? A leprechaun trap? Is he *serious*? When I was a kid, we celebrated St. Patrick's Day by wearing something green. THE END.

The next morning, on St. Patrick's Day, the kids woke up and ran into our room like it was Christmas morning.

Did a leprechaun visit? Can we search for him? Did he leave a pot of gold? Let's go find the gold coins! I bet he left chocolate!

So. Many. Expectations.

All of which were dashed. I did none of those things. I didn't even know I was supposed to *do* those things. As a result, we started that March 17 with four seriously disappointed and grumpy kids. At one point India went into full-blown meltdown mode, kicking random items in her room and yelling about what a LAME HOLIDAY this was.

In my overly tired and increasingly impatient state, I might have yelled back, "YOU'RE RIGHT. This IS a lame holiday. All you do is wear green. And that's all we're doing today. Green. I'm sorry if you do more at school but that's not what we do here. STOP CRYING."

Any holiday defined by wearing a color is a "phone-it-in" holiday, and that's what St. Patrick's Day is supposed to be. Who decided to make it harder for parents? Christmas is enough work already. I don't need another holiday that is hard.

Although, speaking of Christmas . . . according to Pinterest we now have to move an elf around every night into creative tableaus. Because setting up a tree and changing our home decor and hanging lights and buying gifts and sending cards and baking cookies is not enough magic for our precious children.

Meanwhile, Valentine's Day has become the New Halloween, because God forbid you send simple store-bought cards to school with your kids. You'd better include some candy or your child will be shunned. Shunned! One year, one of my kids came home not just with a piece of candy from each kid, but a *whole freaking goodie bag* from each student.

Side note: I would like to speak with the mothers who decided that children who are attending another child's birthday party need to go home with a "goodie bag" *on someone else's birthday.* Why did this become a thing? Did we not have enough to do when we plan a child's birthday? Now we have to fill a bag full of stickers and plastic crap to avoid disappointing children whom we just provided with cake and food and an afternoon in a bounce house?

And Easter. When I was a kid my mom went to the store and bought us a new dress and a premade plastic Easter basket that she put some jelly beans in. It was candy and we loved it. Maybe we would dye some eggs from a kit sitting in the checkout lane at Target that would get all over our hands. They would look like crap. Now we've got to leave footprints from the Easter Bunny and make artful, Pinterest-worthy eggs with stencils and ikat prints and probably some that have glitter. And I hope that dye is nontoxic or better yet, made from plants you foraged.

I refuse to give in to holiday overkill.

Today I made sure all my kids showered. I reminded them to do homework. We sat together at the table and ate a meal that was not procured at a drive-thru. I loaded the dishwasher. I can go big for Christmas and birthdays. That's all I can handle.

I am not judging what other moms do in their homes. You like doing Elf on the Shelf? Great! Knock yourself out. I, too, have been a prime offender at going overboard. (Obnoxious homemade Valentines that look like hipster photo booth strips? Guilty as charged.) But if some of those expectations make you want to lie down and take a nap, it's also okay to opt out. It's okay if your traditions and rituals are understated. Sometimes the need to "do more" is distracting us from the main event: quality time with our kids.

OPTING IN

Happiness comes from living as you need to, as you *want* to. As your inner voice tells you to. Happiness comes from being who you actually are instead of who you think you are supposed to be.

SHONDA RHIMES

I opt out of the aspects of parenting that sap me of my sanity and my energy without paying my family back in connection and love. The beauty of that choice is it provides me with time to focus on things that are really important to us—the things I opt *in to*. Knowing that list of things is just as essential for my sanity. But having values that surface, that you choose to opt in to, are just as important. I say it again because it cannot be over-emphasized in this culture of mommy wars: *The things that are important to me may not be the things that are important to you.*

Here is the list of the things I'm investing in. Yours may be the opposite of mine, and that's okay. Know thyself.

Family Dinners

I am not a morning person and I'm exhausted by the end of the day so sitting down to a meal is the window when I'm most connected with my kids. We sit down to dinner just about every night they are with me. I'm also a stickler about the kids helping with every aspect of the meal. I usually have a kid or two helping me cook and a kid or two helping me clean up, which stretches our dinner routine out to about an hour. I don't mind this. We also totally still do "highs and lows" of our day at every meal, and I don't care how hokey the kids find it. As soon as we sit down, someone will launch into the best and worst parts of their day. I love this connection spot because it cuts through the chitchat, highlights their successes and failures, and invariably leads to great conversations with my kids.

Developing Trust

When my kids were younger, we had an evening tradition of cuddling and reading books. We would read, and then we would just lay and talk. All four in my bed. I've had to get creative now that some of them are teens. Now it's *them* trying to get space away from me. They want to be with their peers, not hanging with Mom. So I work hard to foster conversations, be understanding, and create a soft place to land. We no longer have cuddle sessions in my bed, but about once a week we do huddle up on my bed for what we call "circle of trust." It is both a covenant and an activity. If we have a "circle of trust" meeting it means we are all gonna sit on my bed and share things that we take seriously. It's the space where anyone can talk about anything and it can't leave the room. The amazing thing is that they do share. They've shared crushes and heartbreaks, friendship drama, and secret goals. In our family, "circle of trust" can be invoked as a sort of protection. It might be announced after sharing something at the dinner table, which means that information has to stay within the family. So far, the result is that my kids have come to me with a lot of hard topics and vulnerability that I never would have shared with my own parents.

Being Nonjudgmental

I want my kids to feel like they can come to me with anything. In order to do this, I've had to hear hard truths, about my kids, and about myself. I've had to be open to discussing sex, porn, drugs. I've had to tell them that though I want them to delay sex until adulthood, they can come to me for birth control. They know that even though I don't want them drinking underage, if they do something stupid, I will pick them up. And they know if there is something I am doing that causes them to feel misunderstood, they can tell me about that, too. That hasn't always been fun, but it's been worth it.

Growing Faith Based in Love, and Not Fear

I want my kids to know their relationship with God is about community with a Creator that loves them, and everyone else. In turn, their primary obligation to that love is to express love to others. We go to church, sometimes. Some of my kids attend youth group, and some don't. We listen to worship music in the car, and sometimes gangster rap. We go to a yearly progressive Christian festival that is full of Bible teaching and Pride flags. I run a local chapter of Beer & Hymns, where we take over a bar and sing sacred songs, in an experience that is both rowdy and reverent. I let my kids experience a wide swath of expressions of faith. They know I am a Jesus fan, and I hope they are, too. The expression of faith in our family hinges on showing love to those around us, not adhering to rules that prove we are "good enough" to earn our salvation.

Investing in Social Justice

I want my kids to be caring and compassionate citizens of the world. That starts with having conversations about injustice and "isms." We've gone to Black Lives Matter marches and Pride parades together as a family. We've done house-building trips. We watch documentaries on global issues. We've taken part in holiday events for local foster kids, and we collect and keep care bags for the homeless. We recycle. We do what we can for the environment. We sponsor children in several countries. It's a delicate balance, teaching kids to help without developing a savior mentality, but I keep working at it.

Chores for All

This one is selfish. I am a stickler when it comes to chores. Someone is helping with dinner. Everyone is helping clean it up. Each kid does their own laundry. On the daily, I'm assigning things like emptying the dishwasher or taking out the trash. It's a part of our family culture and with four kids, I can't imagine life without them helping. I also feel strongly that when my kids leave my house, they need to know how to run their own household—my boys will be as proficient at the care and keeping of a household as my girls.

Clean Before Screen

In the words of David Spade in *Reality Bites,* "If you've got time to lean, you've got time to clean." If my kids want to watch TV or play on their iPads, they've got to clean their rooms first. This simple rule is really the only way I keep any semblance of order in my house. Screen time is basically a dangling carrot to keep their rooms from looking like an episode of *Hoarders*.

Music Education

Remember everything I said about not pushing kids into activities they don't want to do? Well I mean that for everything except music lessons, in which case I'm a pushy stage mom. My kids don't have to be prodigies. I don't need them to be orchestra-ready, but I do make my kids take a music lesson once a week, in the hopes that an instrument or two will spark their interest and commitment. Music has been an invaluable part of my life. Being able to sit down and play something as self-care is a gift I want to pass to them. That "hobby" you learned in your youth that remains a positive coping skill for you as an adult might vary from family to family. In ours it's music.

Being a Separate Person with My Own Feelings, Interests, and Passions

Seeing parents as separate and whole human beings is the first step to children learning empathy. My kids need to understand that I have passions and interests beyond being a mom. I go on trips without them. I play in a cover band. I sneak away and read a book when I can. I brought my laptop to their school Christmas concert because Adele tickets went on sale at the same time and getting good seats and supporting my children were equal priorities. Sometimes I have a podcast playing in my ears while I watch them play soccer. Sometimes I talk on the phone in front of them. It might be an important phone conversation or I might be chatting with friends because I HAVE FRIENDS, TOO, KIDS.

If our lives revolve around our kids, they grow up burdened by the need to make us happy. The more sources of fulfillment we have besides them, the more we liberate our kids.

. . .

Sometimes I mess up. Sometimes I fail at even the things I'm trying to make space for. I've missed a school concert whose flyer was on my fridge for a month just because I forgot. I've submitted the wrong baby photo into the yearbook for one of my kids, who immediately noticed. I've been late. I've been too sarcastic. I've broken their trust. I've yelled. I've shamed. I've worked on giving myself grace to be human, even with my kids, and I let them into that struggle. I apologize. I admit when I'm wrong. I listen when I've hurt them. I think that allowing my kids to see my imperfections is helpful. It gives them permission to make their own mistakes. It allows me to model what it looks like to own your own crap and apologize.

A part of being a "good enough" mom is letting my kids be "good enough" kids. It's allowing them to make their own mistakes. It's letting them fail instead of micromanaging their lives. It's about allowing them to face natural consequences instead of covering them in bubble wrap. It's about not requiring them to be perfect in terms of grades or sports or achievements. I want my kids to feel the freedom to excel at any of their passions, but I also want them to feel the freedom to be average. I'm trying to emphasize "being" over "doing." In a culture where we are constantly hearing "you were made for more," I want to teach them "you are enough."

IT GETS BETTER: THE LIGHT AT THE END OF THE LAUNDRY ROOM

Thus the mother-child relationship is paradoxical and, in a sense, tragic. It requires the most intense love on the mother's side, yet this very love must help the child grow away from the mother, and to become fully independent.

ERICH FROMM

The struggle of the human experience, from a parenting standpoint, is that we spend years longing for the freedom of the future—potty training, independent kids, simplified travel, empty nests—until those things actually arrive. Then we pine for the good old days when our children needed us. It feels like I'm always on the verge of the next big milestone, and always ready for it to get here as soon as possible. But when that next stage arrives, it brings along a little sadness, because I also lose something. Transition always leaves something lovely behind, and in the immortal words of the great '80s glam metal band Cinderella, you don't know what you got till it's gone.

This year I have one kid in high school and two in middle

school. My youngest, now in fifth grade, is growing up so fast she probably already has her own YouTube channel I don't know about. Childhood seems to take forever until you're a parent. Then it takes, like, two weeks and suddenly they're showing you their new tattoos and helping you fix the Wi-Fi and the whole childhood thing is *done*.

I'm wavering between excitement and sadness. Between optimism and deep, sinking woe. I long to see my children reach milestones and I find myself on the bathroom floor ugly-crying when it finally happens. The parenting paradox.

I love watching my kids grow up and turn into developed human beings with unique personalities, perspectives, and interests. They are beginning to figure out who they are, and what is emerging is just so lovely I could bawl.

Jafta is six feet tall. He looks like he's eighteen but he's astoundingly sentimental and sweet. He cracks me up on the regular with his biting wit and sarcasm. He loves skateboarding and puts more effort into an outfit than anyone in the family. He has a great ear for music and plays both bass and guitar. He plays in the worship band at church and listens to rap music with filthy lyrics that I pretend to be scandalized by but secretly like.

India is . . . well, she's me. So much like me that I don't know whether to celebrate it or stage an intervention. She loves making lists and getting shit done. She's a social justice advocate and natural leader ready to take on the world. At thirteen, she's schooling me for using noninclusive language. She never met a book she didn't like, and she can recite the lyrics to just about any musical written in the last decade. She's currently planning a solo trip to New York, an idea she presented to me using a multimedia presentation she worked on for a week. She is Leslie Knope personified. At age twelve she has already mapped out her route between the design college she will attend and her Google office where she will be a Web designer.

Kembe is a charmer. He's got a million-dollar smile and is an eternal optimist. He is positive and cheerful and always encouraging the people around him. He's the favorite among the younger boys at his school because he's always ready with a high five or knuckles, and makes everyone else feel important. He's phenomenally good at every sport he tries. His social skills and confidence are a thing to behold.

Karis is our self-appointed comedian. She marches to the beat of her own drum, which may have been inevitable being the youngest sibling of three big personalities. She's assertive but endearing, empathic, sensitive, and incredibly creative. She can take a gum wrapper and an old sock and somehow make it into an outfit for her doll. She is quirky and hilarious and confident in who she is. She's also a budding theater geek and made me bawl singing "Seasons of Love" at her school talent show all by herself.

I don't just love these kids, I like them. I want to be friends with them. Not in a "cool mom" way, trying to be besties with my kid by being some kind of permissive peer. I genuinely want to be around them, want to do things with them, and want to be someone they trust and confide in.

We have our long-standing "circle of trust" tradition, but lately I've been joking about a second "circle of trust" that refers to the sixty-mile circumference around our house where it is permissible for them to attend college. Surprisingly, I am turning into the mom who cannot bear the thought of her children moving away for college. I went away to college my freshman year, and never returned. I'd love to have my kids stay close, but I have to support them if they choose to leave. Again, that critical balancing act of being able to hold two things as true when it comes to parenting: accepting my own feelings as valid, but not letting my own feelings create fences that barricade my kids' dreams. Still, I will secretly hold out hope that all four of them land their adult lives within driving distance of my house. Because, man, I really like being with them.

Unlike when they were toddlers, when I was starved for time away from them, these days I find myself wanting more time than I actually get. They are consumed with texting and friends and their social lives, but we still manage to find genuine pleasure in each other's company. We have fun watching *The Daily Show* together. We pore over cookbooks and plan meals together. We laze on the couch and share stories from our days. As opposed to when they were toddlers, if I imagined them as adult roommates now I would actually think they were really cool. A little on the messy side, but still cool.

It's not perfect. I could do with less grumbling and I'd love to stop giving so many reminders to put shoes way. Teenagers dazzle you and push you, at the same time. This weekend, I had a kid mow the whole yard *without being asked.* I had another kid make chicken marsala *from scratch.* And those same kids, in the same week, lied to my face, tried to get around my Internet filters, and there might have been a grounding over a vape pen.

My kids are, to use a little Christianese, "between the Already and the Not Yet." They can be delightful, competent, amazing adults, and self-centered, devious little shits. That is the universal experience of parenting someone who is already grown in so many ways and not yet adult in so many others. You feel as if you are friends who understand each other one day, and as if they have betrayed you or bewildered you the next.

My biggest challenge at this stage is learning to differentiate from them as they weather the storms of their own lives. It's been said that having a child means having your heart walk around in someone else's body, and I feel that keenly. It is a genuine struggle for me to resist feeling every single feeling that my kids are experiencing . . . their hurts, their triumphs, their struggles, their heartbreaks. I'm not saying this in a humble-brag "look at what a sensitive and in-tune mother I am" way. I'm saying that if I'm not careful, I have an unhealthy enmeshment with my kids' feelings and moods. Case in point: One of my kids had a heartbreak this week and I have cried about it five times. *Five.* No one broke up with me but I am crying. Because that makes sense. I feel like my experiences of motherhood taught me to let go of trying to control my own outcomes, but just as I learned to do that, I found that my heart holds the outcomes of my children's lives in a death grip. Perhaps that is my next big lesson.

Using that roller-coaster metaphor, my friend Jen Hatmaker talks about how, in raising older kids, we've got to stay on the platform. We cannot ride every roller coaster with them. We need to stay right there, calm and anchored on the platform, and be a stable force for when they get off. That is my entire goal for the next eight years. To stay on the motherf***ing platform until they leave home.

Nothing in my life has been more stressful than being a mother. Nothing has been more joyous. It's the hardest thing and best thing I've ever done. And yet, I'm keenly aware that I've been following in the footsteps of generations of women who knew that same deep happiness and that same mind-numbing exhaustion. The specifics of the stories I've told here—the miscarriages; the long, frustrating fight to adopt two amazing boys; the pregnancies that brought two incredible girls; the divorce—those details are mine. The feelings behind the stories—hope and crushing disappointment; exhaustion and resentment; wonder and worry; gratitude and uncertainty—those are universal. I didn't write this book to tell you about one woman's life, or one family's story. I wrote it because even now, after so many decades of progress, motherhood gets bubble-wrapped in myth and shrouded in platitudes. Those myths and platitudes leave too many moms feeling isolated, worn out, and convinced there's something wrong with them.

The more we can tell our truths, *especially* the hard and uncomfortable ones, the less alone and broken we'll feel. Perhaps there is less wrong with us, and more wrong with the expectations we've put upon ourselves. Perhaps we're good enough, just as we are.

ACKNOWLEDGMENTS

Thank you to Jafta, Kembe, India, and Karis. In the midst of the sarcasm, I hope this reads as a love letter to the adventure of being your mom. It's been the best ride of my life, and I'm so grateful every day that I get to live life with such insanely awesome human beings. I love you, and I like you.

Thank you to Rachel Held Evans for showing me what bravery looks like, and for cheering me on as I wrote this book. I miss you.

Thank you to Chad Markley for keeping the wheels on for the past two years. You were my sanity and my emotional-support person, and often the only reason the kids ate dinner. Thank you for loving us so well.

Thank you to Tara Livesay, Jamie Wright, Jen Hatmaker, Sarah Goodfellow, and Sarah Bessey for helping me structure this book, for constantly encouraging me, and for listening to my incessant whining about how I wanted to quit writing altogether. But more important, thank you for being my tribe of elephants for the parts of life that were actually much harder than writing this book. Your friendship has been a lifeboat, and I feel so lucky to have you.

Thanks to SFB for bringing your weird and special brand of humor, love, encouragement, and irreverence into my life on a regular basis.

Thanks to Jason Boyett, Matthew Paul Turner, Ed Cyweski, Cara Meredith, Hugo Schwyzer, Jennifer Cretu, and Jillian Lauren for reading my early drafts and setting me in the right direction, to David Drury for chapter-title inspiration, and to Kelley Nikondeha for setting deadlines for me and holding me to them. Thanks to Robin Plemmons for illustrating my life into a time line. F.A.Y.

Thank you to my agent, Margaret Riley King, for your undying patience, and for believing in me even as I was dragging my feet. Thank you to my editor, Mary Reynics, for shaping a very long first draft blob of words into a cohesive book. Your keen eye and wisdom made this book exponentially better.

Thank you to Sarah James for being my self-care mentor as I wrote this book. Thanks to my sisterwives Claire and Anna—you are the friends and neighbors I imagined being surrounded by when I thought of motherhood. Thank you for yelling at my kids when they need it and for being a second home for them.

Thank you to David Kopp and Frank Schaeffer for being my longtime encouragers, and for not dropping the subject of when I was going to write a book for most of the past decade. You believed in me long before I believed in myself.

Thank you to my OG blog readers . . . the ones who were reading back when it was called "The Howerton Family Blog" . . . the ones who put up with annoying sponsored posts and rants about things I didn't like and entirely too many recaps of *The Bachelor.* I've always felt my readers were an amazing community and I've loved dialoguing with you over the years.

And last but certainly not least, thank you to my launch team, who helped shape so many aspects of the finalization of this book. That clever line on the back-jacket copy? Was probably their idea.

ABOUT THE AUTHOR

KRISTEN HOWERTON is a licensed marriage and family therapist and became the mother of four children within four years via birth and adoption. She is the founder of the blog Rage Against the Minivan, where, in the midst of writing about the raw emotions and experience of motherhood, she has become a fierce advocate for social justice, orphan care, and helping fellow parents to step up to hard conversations about race with their kids. Howerton has created several popular humor destinations online, including the Tumblr "Pinterest, You Are Drunk" and the #assholeparent meme and Instagram account. She is the co-host of *Selfie,* a podcast dedicated to exploring the mind, body, and spirit aspects of self-care.

rageagainsttheminivan.com
Facebook.com/kristenhowerton
Twitter: @kristenhowerton
Instagram: @rageagainsttheminivan
and @kristenhowerton
Pinterest.com/kristenhowerton

ABOUT THE TYPE

This book was set in Minion, a 1990 Adobe Originals typeface by Robert Slimbach (b. 1956). Minion is inspired by classical, old-style typefaces of the late Renaissance, a period of elegant, beautiful, and highly readable type designs. Created primarily for text setting, Minion combines the aesthetic and functional qualities that make text type highly readable with the versatility of digital technology.